Building Jaipur

Building Jaipur

The Making of an Indian City

VIBHUTI SACHDEV AND GILES TILLOTSON

REAKTION BOOKS

Published by
REAKTION BOOKS LTD
79 Farringdon Road
London ECIM 3JU, UK

www.reaktionbooks.co.uk

Printed and bound in Hong Kong

British Library Cataloguing in Publication Data

Sachdev, Vibhuti
    Building Jaipur : the making of an Indian city
    1. Architecture - India - Jaipur - History 2.Architecture, Modern
    3.Jaipur (India) - Buildings, structures, etc.
    I. Title II. Tillotson, Giles
    720.9'544

ISBN 1 86189 1377

Published with the assistance of the Getty Grant Program.

Contents

Preface and Acknowledgements

Architecture throughout the world in recent decades has experienced a changing relationship with its past. The collapse of confidence in Modernism as a panacea, as the ready and reliable solution, came from its tendency to universalize at the expense of local and particular needs, felt especially by architecture's users, and from the loss of diversity in expression. In some extreme cases the desire to recover regional or historical elements has led into atavism; but more often the attempt has been to graft onto the continuing mainstream selected elements of restored identities. Hence the variety of Post-Modernisms, and the 'abstract' or 'critical' regionalism, that are by now commonplace. These new approaches are often highly sensitive to the forms, the textures and even the materials of historical or regional building systems. But for the most part the borrowed qualities are rationalized afresh, they are redefined within the context of a Post-Modern philosophy; and there has been some reluctance to engage with the organizing logic – with the *theory* – of those original systems. Considered archaic or arcane – or just complicated and forgotten – theories from the past are often quietly passed over in favour of some 'essence', which may in truth be rather sketchily defined, but which is offered as easy to grasp and applicable to the needs of the present. Extending beyond a debate amongst professionals about appropriate procedures, all of this deeply affects members of the wider public, with whom architects must communicate. This book addresses this pressing global issue, taking as the ground for discussion the development from pre-colonial to Post-Modern India.

We begin with the past. In pre-modern India indigenous architectural design was governed by a broad but distinctive body of theory known by the Sanskrit term *vastu vidya* ('architectural knowledge'). It was never static or uncompromising (as some now think), but as it developed over time it provided a consistent logical structure within which to conceptualize design. As architecture has evolved in India over the past 150 years, in response to British colonial and post-colonial policies, *vastu vidya* has become increasingly marginalized and fragmented, decreasingly practised and understood. There are of course some patchy survivals, and lately there have even been some high-profile revivals (which we will address), but if anything these make the situation worse: precisely because they are partial and misguided they tend to make a true perception of historical *vastu vidya* even harder to achieve. One consequence of this is a severe limitation placed upon our comprehension of the architecture of the past, a central element of India's cultural heritage. How can we claim to know historical buildings if we can describe them only in our own terms, ignoring the rationale of their architects? The many surviving texts which (along with historical buildings) embody this lost knowledge are not much studied by architects or even by architectural historians, for whom they are rendered seemingly inaccessible by their language (notably Sanskrit) and by the decontextualization of their information. Correspondingly, efforts to interpret the texts by expert linguists commonly founder on these specialists' lack of architectural knowledge. An approach that combines these specialisms is long overdue. Despite a few exceptions, the current state of Indian architectural historiography falls well short of this. Why does this matter? Well, although cross-cultural comparisons are hazardous, we might indicate what is being missed by pointing out that no one today would seriously attempt to describe the Classical architecture of Europe without a full appreciation of its many articulations in writing from Vitruvius onwards. Imagine a world in which we knew nothing but a few half-remembered scraps of Arabic astronomy, or of Chinese medicine. With Indian architecture we have such a world: a whole creative structure of human thought is lost, buried under the rubble of what came after, and it will require much intellectual archaeology to reveal what it once was. One aim of this book is to indicate by example what a more integrated approach to Indian architectural history might look like.

Such an approach will have significance not only for how we understand the past, and how we conserve it, but also for how we use it. The book's second and related aim is to assess what influence a deeper understanding of *vastu vidya* might exert on future practice, and to consider by comparison those various partial and fragmentary uses to which it is already being put today. For in spite of its eclipse by Modern methods and its near complete exclusion from the educational system, *vastu vidya*

is not wholly extinct. Ill-digested fragments of it are revived, for example by some leading Indian architects in their sincere attempts to bridge the gulf between Modern and traditional paradigms; other elements of it form the armoury of self-styled '*vastu* consultants', whose services have increasingly been sought in recent years by householders and businessmen (in a process broadly analogous to some of the current applications of *feng shui*); and there is even some evidence of the continuous survival of *vastu* expertise amongst India's largely disenfranchised architectural craftsmen. All of these currents could claim to have value in a society where communication by means of a regional vocabulary is earnestly desired; but in every case the application is superficial. A deeper understanding of the historical role of *vastu vidya* will facilitate a critique of its contemporary uses, and form the basis for a further original argument about its future potential. At the end of the book we shall argue that *vastu vidya* could have a positive role to play in new design, albeit in ways perhaps not yet attempted. It may be emphasized at the outset that this argument does not proceed from any sentimental wish to see the restoration of archaic imagery in building design – it is not about *style* at all – but rather from a reasoned analysis of the comparative powers of Modernist and of indige-nous systems of architectural logic to establish effective communication between architects and the societies that they serve. The argument is based on a conception of 'tradition' not as a static state but as a process of change in which the wider society participates.

To provide a central core to a wide topic, our method is to focus the analysis on a single site, and to treat it as a test case. For this purpose we have selected the city of Jaipur. There are many reasons why Jaipur recommends itself as a suitable choice for such a treatment. To begin with, it is one of the most famous cities in India. With a resident population now in excess of one and a half million, it is also highly popular amongst both domestic and foreign tourists, who are attracted by its living craft traditions, its palaces and the regularly planned walled city at its core. Founded in the early eighteenth century, it is pre-colonial in inception – designed sufficiently recently to ensure the ready availability of ample source material, yet in accordance with indigenous principles. Standing on the cusp between the late medieval and the modern worlds, the early eighteenth century was a period of rapid economic and political change, which thus presents some challenging comparisons with our own times. Moving ahead to the British colonial period, Jaipur is again especially interesting because it remained the capital of a semi-autonomous Indian state that lay outside the domain of British India. The relationship with the central power was more subtle than that of regions under direct British control, and in the field of architecture this gave rise – as we shall see – to some potentially instructive initiatives. In the years since Independence, Jaipur, now the capital of Rajasthan, has experienced rapid and dramatic expansion, and contributions to this process have been made by some of India's leading modern architects, including B.V. Doshi and Charles Correa. It is perhaps only the combination of all these factors that makes Jaipur exceptional, and in none of the circumstances described is it unique; thus at each successive stage of its history it can be used to exemplify much wider developments. It also happens to be a city with which both the authors have enjoyed a familiarity, through regular visits, for over twenty years.

Jaipur, then, provides the main but not exclusive focus of our four central chapters, which together present a synoptic history of Indian architectural theory over the last three centuries, a period that saw the gradual shift from the dominance of the indigenous paradigm to the challenging perceptions of the present. The significance of what we may learn from this test case, for scholarship, for conservation, for 'vastu consultancy' and for future design are matters that we take up in much more general terms in our final chapter. But we begin, also with a wider perspective, by defining some of the outlines of a vastu vidya conception of what a city might be.

The research on which this study is based was supported by a major grant from the Arts and Humanities Research Board in 1999–2000. Seed funding and supplementary grants were awarded by the Charles Wallace India Trust, the SOAS Research and Publications Committees and the University of London Convocation. We are grateful for this support. We also wish to thank the following individuals and institutions for permission to reprint images: Catherine B. Asher (illus. 6); Charles Correa (illus. 105, 106, 118); Vera Röhm (illus. 40, 41); the Maharaja Sawai Man Singh II Museum, Jaipur (illus. 7, 23, 34); B. V. Doshi and Marg Publications, Mumbai (illus. 103, 104); the Royal Asiatic Society, London (illus. 5, 22, 32, 44, 74); and the Victoria & Albert Museum, London (illus. 25). All other unattributed drawings and photographs are by the authors.

In Jaipur, our thanks are due to Kunwar Narendra Singh, Shri Yaduendra Sahai, Dr Naval Krishna, Miss Manvi Sharma and Dr Rima Hooja. And in London, to Dr Rupert Snell and the team at Reaktion.

1 Vishvakarma, the divine architect.

1 Conceptual Cities

IN pre-colonial India, ideas about kingship and about cities were never static; indeed, their development over time could in itself provide an interesting area of enquiry. But as a preliminary to our case study we have here chosen to focus on a few salient elements that were consistently present in definitions of kingship and of cities up until the eighteenth century. We have drawn chiefly on two related genres of literature. The first is *niti shastra*, or treatises on politics and statecraft. Here we have used in particular the ancient classic of the genre, the *Arthashastra*, composed during the Mauryan period (fourth to third centuries BC) and well known ever since, and – to give a more contemporary perspective – the late derivative work the *Sukraniti*. The second genre is *vastu shastra*, treatises that deal with architecture, planning and all other aspects of design. Here again our sources include two early classics, the *Manasara* and the *Mayamata*, and also two later works – the *Samrangana Sutradhara*, written in the eleventh century for Raja Bhoja of Dhar, and Mandan's *Rajavallabha*, written in the fifteenth century for Rana Kumbha of Mewar – whose northern provenance and Rajput patronage put them closer to our case study of Jaipur. The question of the relationship between the ideas contained in such texts and actual historical practice is touched on here but is considered more fully in later chapters.

The Shastric King

Time is divided into seasons, says the author of the *Sukraniti*, because of changes in the atmospheric conditions which cause rains, cold and heat to succeed one another, and because of changes in the astronomical conditions, according to the movement, shape and nature of the planets. But time is equally divided, he continues, by the deeds of men, whether beneficial or harmful, great or small. Conduct is the cause of time. This must be so, for if it were the other way round, and the time or epoch were the cause of men's actions, how could we attribute virtue to those actions? Now, since it is the king who makes the rules and establishes customs, both by imposing them on his subjects and by following them himself, it is the king who is responsible for guiding men's conduct. The king is therefore the cause or maker of time.[1]

Following the customary preamble and insistence on the importance of his theme, this is the first point of substance made by the author of the *Sukraniti*, a Sanskrit treatise on polity, of uncertain date.[2] In linking the king to the cosmic order, and attributing to him a power comparable to that of the planets, the author is assuming familiarity with the more general idea of the king as a representative, even an embodiment, of god.[3] A little later he lists the eight functions of the king as punishing the wicked, dispensing charity, protecting his subjects, performing rites and sacrifices, acquiring revenue, converting independent princes into tributary chiefs, conquering enemies and generating wealth from the land.[4] The king must keep himself informed on the well-being of his subjects, as dispraise can do him much harm – after all, it was the criticism of a mere washerman that led Rama to forsake Sita.[5]

The king who is most praised is one who is educated in the arts and sciences, because if he is trained in all branches of learning he will not incline to wrong deeds and will earn the respect of the good. The logic of this idea implies a contract: the identification of the king as a god confers upon him not only privileges but also duties to behave in certain ways and to acquire certain qualities. Each and every one of his actions – including his engagement in *puja* (prayer and ritual) and his patronage of learning – is measured against what is expected of a king. Therefore the king should revere his *guru* (or personal preceptor) and through association with him acquire knowledge of the *shastras* (the canonical treatises). More than this, he should take steps to advance the arts and sciences amongst his people, by regularly honouring those who are well versed in all sacred texts such as *vedas* and *puranas*, and those who understand astrology, medicine and sacred rites, including *tantra*.[6]

Respect for the *guru* is a point equally stressed by the author of the *Manasara*, a treatise not on *niti* (statecraft) but on *vastu shastra* (architecture and design).[7] The *Manasara* goes on to define nine ranks of kings, from the most powerful Chakravartin, ruler of a kingdom which extends to the four oceans, through a Maharaja, king of seven kingdoms, and the Narendra who is king of three, all the way down to the Astragrahin, the lord of a single fort. The nine ranks are distinguished not only by the size of their domains but also by their

personal qualities and by the proportion of the kingdom's revenue they receive.[8] The distinctive qualities of the Maharaja, for example, are that he is born of the solar or lunar race, that he is well versed in politics and ethics, and that he holds 'three-fold royal powers . . . is aware of the six royal policies, [and] possesses six kingly strengths'. That the author does not pause to itemize these powers, policies and strengths is a clear indication that he regarded his text as a contribution to a wider body of knowledge: he can omit to specify what these phrases mean, by assuming that his readers would already be familiar with them from other sources. And the assumption would be fair. The most famous Indian work on statecraft, the *Arthashastra* of Kautilya, for example, defines royal power as three-fold, comprising the power of knowledge through counsel (*mantra*), the power of majesty through the treasury and the army (*prabhava*) and the power of energy through valour (*utsaha*).[9] The same source and the equally famous *Manusmriti* both tell us that the six tactics of foreign policy are making alliances, waging war, marching, camping, taking shelter and being duplicitous.[10] And both texts define the strength of the state as depending on seven constituent elements, including the king and his six supports: his minister, the country, the fortified city, the treasury, the army and the ally.[11]

Some other major *vastu shastra* texts, including the *Aparajita Priccha* and the *Rajavallabha*, have their own rankings of kings, comparable to that of the *Manasara*, though with some variation in their number and names.[12] We might reasonably wonder what purpose all this classification serves. The texts do not agree with each other, and none corresponds to an actual hierarchy known to have existed at any particular historical moment. So the lists are most certainly not schedules of protocol. Rather, their purpose appears to be to insist that distinctions between kings of different levels can be made on the basis of their kingdoms and their qualities, and that the lesser kings must not usurp the functions and attributes of superior ones; and they do this not by describing any given actual hierarchy but by defining an ideal or conceptual one, against which real hierarchies can be measured. The point of this device is to place the orders made by men within the larger context of superhuman ones, for the scale ends with the Chakravartin, whose domain extends to the four mythical oceans at the ends of the world – a kingdom that has never yet been achieved. The list of qualities that define a Maharaja is not an empirical description of the attributes of any individuals, but a definition of the quality of power to which it is proper for a Maharaja – and only a Maharaja – to aspire. If the texts do not describe kingship in the world, neither do they prescribe what it might realistically become. Instead, they illustrate the principles of real kingship by offering ideal images of their perfect fulfilment. And they adopt, as we shall see, precisely the same approach to their principal topic: planning.

The Shastric City

No fewer than eight distinct types of city and town (and a further eight types of fort) are defined by the *Manasara* and another major *vastu shastra* text, the *Mayamata*. In this instance we are confronted not with a hierarchy but with specialisms, and the first on the list, far from being way off any realizable register, is in fact a basic or standard type whose very name, *kevala nagara*, means 'only' or 'ordinary'. A densely populated mercantile town, the *kevala nagara* is protected by a wall with a gate at each of the four cardinal points. It is the second on the list that is the *rajadhani* or *rajadhaniya*

nagara, the royal capital. This is defined as a city, impregnable on the north and east sides, with the royal palace near the centre and a guard facing towards the east and the south, and around the palace the houses of people of all classes, including the most wealthy and meritorious citizens of the state. A *pura*, by contrast, lacks the palace and the emphasis is on trade. A *kheta* is a town situated close to a river or a mountain, and is exclusively inhabited by members of the Shudra caste; a *kharvata* is a town within the hills; and a *kubjaka* is an unprotected town located between a *kheta* and a *kharvata*. A *pattana* is a trading town situated by the coast or a waterway, and a *shibira* is a fortified town, protecting the kingdom's border. The eight forts have similarly specialist functions and are distinguished by location, population and the presence or absence of the king.[13]

The location of some of these forts and cities is already implied in their definitions, but beyond this is the idea that the best site is one to which can be attributed some sacred association – a site that may be identified with a legend, or as the scene of some action of a god. All associations of the site will be borne by the city and will influence its fortunes. Before building can commence, offerings must be made to propitiate the gods and demons.[14]

Once the site is selected and purified, the laying out of the plan involves referring to a set of diagrams. The chapters on planning in the *vastu shastras* describe a sequence of 32 *mandalas*, a set of grids of increasing complexity. The first and simplest is a single square – notionally a 1 x 1 grid. The second is a square subdivided into four equal parts – a 2 x 2 grid. The third has nine parts, the fourth sixteen, and so on, until the last, 32 x 32, or 1024-square grid. These are the *vastu purusha mandalas*, the elementary principles for any division of space (illus. 2).[15] All of the subsequent chapters

Paja

North

Charaki

Roga knee	Naga left arm	Mukhya left arm	Bhallata left arm	Kubera left arm	Shaila left arm	Aditi shoulder	Diti ear	Isha head
Papayakshama shank	Rudra left hand		Prithvidhara breast			Apavtsa heart		Parjanya ear
Shesha shank	Rudradasa left hand					Apah neck		Jaya shoulder
Asura shank								Indra right arm
Varuna shank	Maitra thigh		Brahma head, navel, back			Aryama breast		Surya right arm
Pushpadanta shank								Satya right arm
Sugriva shank	Jaya genitals		Vivasvat thigh			Savita right hand		Bhrisha right arm
Nandi shank	Indra genitals					Savitra right hand		Akasha right arm
Pitri feet	Mriga shank	Bhringa shank	Gandharva shank	Yama shank	Grihakshata shank	Vitatha shank	Pusha shank	Agni knee

West   East

Puteraka

South

Vidanka

2 The *paramashayika*, or 8 x 8 square *vastu purusha mandala*, drawn according the definition of the *Rajavallabha*.

on specific constructions – whether single houses or temples, palaces, villages or towns – refer back to the types thus defined. No fixed dimension is attached to any *mandala*, and we should not suppose that the more complex versions are necessarily intended for larger works. They are primary planning forms that can be used in any context.

The *Mayamata* says that for any town it is appropriate to use the four-square *mandala* (called *pechaka*) or the 100-square *mandala* (called *asana*) or any of those in between; that is to say, anything from a 2 x 2 to a 10 x 10 grid, thus excluding the first in the sequence as too simple, and all of the more complex forms.[16] The *Manasara* roughly agrees: identifying the lines of the grid with the city's main streets, it says that the number of streets running from west to east and from north to south may be anything between one and twelve.[17] Two later *vastu shastra* texts are much more specific. The *Samrangana Sutradhara* says that the 64-square *mandala* (called *chandita*) is appropriate for all towns; and the *Rajavallabha* recommends the same model for use in cities, palaces and villages.[18]

The widths of the streets within a town, and of one town compared with another, vary according to a strict hierarchy. It is not appropriate for a small town to have streets of the greatest width. An ordinary town, according to the *Mayamata*, can have as many as 13 separate street widths, increasing in increments of half a *danda*, from 1 to 7 *danda*.[19] Almost all the texts speak of a principal street or group of streets called *rajmarg* (or royal highway), which runs through the centre of the town and connects with the palace. Although for general use, these are also intended for the movement of troops and must be *pucca* (paved).[20] As might be expected, the political treatises such as the *Arthashastra* and the *Sukraniti* also have much to say about the *rajmargs*, and are especially emphatic about their proper maintenance. For throwing dirt on a road, says the *Arthashastra*, the fine is one eighth of a *pana*; for blocking it with muddy water, a quarter of a *pana*; but on a *rajmarg* these fines are doubled. For excreting faeces by a royal property, the fine is as much as four *pana*, twice the amount due if the offence is committed by a public well; but the fines are halved if only urine is passed, and waived altogether if the offence is due to sickness or fear.[21] The author of the *Sukraniti* advises the king to pass a law prohibiting the obstruction of all roads, temples, wells, parks and boundaries, and to permit the free movement of the poor, the blind and the crippled.[22]

The construction of temples within the town is also a responsibility of the king (illus. 3). Whatever his own personal affiliation, he must build and maintain temples to all of the gods and join with the people in the celebration of their festivals.[23] The *Manasara* goes so far as to specify particular districts within the town for each of the principal deities; but it is consistent with the other *vastu shastras* in

3 A general view of Amber showing royal temples.

insisting that a royal capital must have a Vishnu temple at its centre.[24] All the temples face east or west, or towards the town centre, and a temple outside the town must not have its back towards it.[25]

In a town or city intended for a general population including all four castes, the distribution of the people is systematic. The district where each citizen resides and works is determined by his caste and occupation. The standard pattern is the one described in the *Samrangana Sutradhara*, which places Brahmins in the north, Kshatriyas in the east, Vaishyas in the south and Shudras in the west.[26] Detail is added to this broad distribution by reference to the associations of the deities who govern each of the subdivisions of the *mandala*. For example, the south-eastern corner of the *mandala* is attributed to Agni, the god of fire; and accordingly the south-eastern corner of the city is reserved for those who work with fire, such as blacksmiths and cooks. The north-western corner, by contrast, is assigned to Vayu, the god of wind; and this direction is accordingly preferred for trades which involve movement, such as keeping carriages or being a shepherd.[27] Each of the bazaars is allocated to a particular plot of the *mandala* according to the type of produce sold.[28] The system is elegant but not so rigidly drawn as to defy utility, and the texts are equally insistent that all costly goods such as gems, gold and fine textiles should be sold on the central streets leading to the palace, and that flowers and incense should be sold in shops located outside the temples.[29]

The Shastric Palace

The centre of the *mandala* is the *brahmasthana*, its most sacred zone, presided over by Brahma himself. When the *mandala* is employed in the construction of a temple, the *brahmasthana* corresponds to the *garbha griha*, the image chamber at the temple's core (illus. 17). In city planning, as we have seen, it is the ideal location for a Vishnu temple. The palace of the king is normally located to the west, but some texts allow that the centre may also be used for the palace, and the *Mayamata* even suggests that this is a prerogative of the highest class of king.[30]

The shastric conception of a palace is of a series of concentric enclosures or courts. Their number depends on the rank of the king. The most elaborate palace, with seven enclosures, is reserved for the Chakravartin, while a Maharaja may have up to six, a Narendra up to five and, at the bottom of the scale, the Astragrahin will have to be content with a maximum of two. The relative proportions of the courtyards are also determined. If the central court is considered as a square with a side of one unit, then the second, which encloses it, will be three units across; the third will be seven units; the fourth, thirteen units; the fifth, 21 units; the sixth, 31 units; and the seventh, 34 or 40 units (illus. 18).[31]

The outer courtyards are intended for storage, for the stabling of animals and for the more public functions of the king, while the inner courtyards are reserved for his private residence and the apartments of his queens. Beyond this, each of the courts is considered as a *mandala*, following on a smaller scale precisely the same model that structures the city as a whole. Thus each courtyard is conceptually divided into directions and zones, with each division being assigned to the appropriate deity, and assigned a function accordingly. In a palace of three enclosures, according to the *Manasara* for example, the north-eastern corner of the inner enclosure houses the king's dining hall, while the same corner of the second enclosure has a temple (reflecting the special association of this direction with *puja* and contemplation), and the north-east section of the third enclosure accommodates the cowsheds, with

4 The palace of Amber, from above.

5 Maharaja Sawai Jai Singh II.

6 Shri Govind, with
Radha, installed in the
Govind Deo temple at
Jaipur.

7 Painted map of
Jaipur; 18th century.

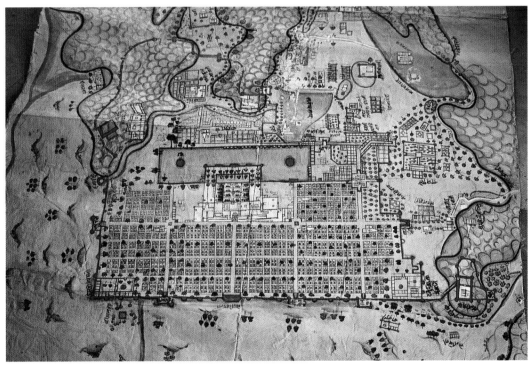

8 The view westwards across the city, from the direction of Galta.

9 Sanganeri Gate.

10 Part of the front of a *haveli* in Jaipur.

11 Part of the city wall of Jaipur.

12 Bathing *kunda* at the pilgrimage centre at Galta.

13 The Naqqarwal ka Darwaza.

14 The Ganesh Pol, in the courtyard of the Sarvato Bhadra.

15 Part of a doorway in the Pritam Niwas Chowk, the courtyard before the Chandra Mahal.

16 View northwards down Sireh Deori Bazaar, from the summit of the Hawa Mahal.

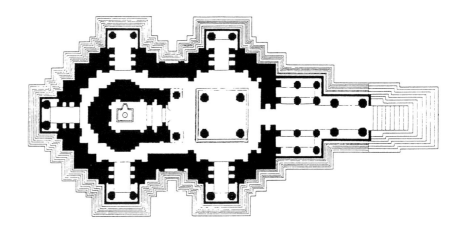

17 Plan of the 11th-century Kandariya Mahadev temple at Khajuraho, built by the Chandella Rajputs.

their entrances facing outwards, towards the east. In the south-west of the inner enclosure are found the queens' apartments, and in the corresponding part of the second is the audience hall. The arsenal is located slightly to the north of west in the inner enclosure, and the apartment of the king's son in the corresponding part of the second enclosure. On the northern side of the palace we should find the concubines' house in the inner enclosure, a flower garden and dancing court in the second and a pavilion for cockfights in the outer enclosure.[32]

If the various texts which specify such details are not always consistent with each other,[33] this is not because the authors are employing different systems but because they are applying it in subtly different ways. It is not the particular apartments whose positions are agreed but those of the deities of the *mandala*. The secondary matters of those deities' associations, and of what palace functions are most appropriately assigned to them, are open to individual interpretation. But they all agree that the outermost area of the palace should have a stone or brick protective wall, with guards (implying entrances) stationed on the east and south sides.[34]

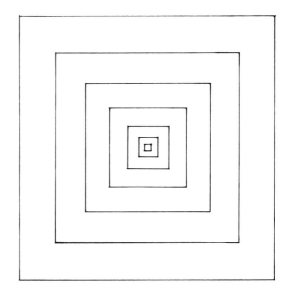

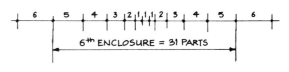

18 Concentric zones of a palace, drawn according to the description in the *Manasara*.

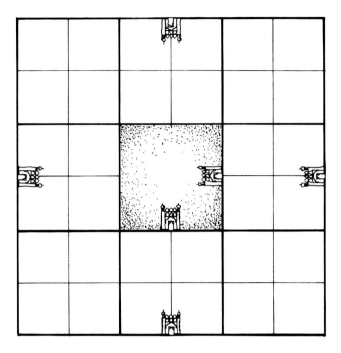

19 A paradigmatic
capital city, drawn
according to general
shastric definition.

Shastra and Archaeology

The process of rendering shastric ideas
diagrammatically is hazardous, if one visual
realization is presumed to exclude others, since in
practice many are possible. But taking the
definitions of city and palace given above, one
possible rendering of a paradigmatic capital city
would be as in illus. 19. If the texts define
paradigms, it might reasonably be asked why in the
archaeological record there are few, if any, actual
towns that closely correspond to them. The
apparent discrepancy between the shastric idea of a
town and those that have been built has led many to
question the role of *vastu shastra* in the history of
Indian architecture as a whole, and in the
construction of Jaipur in particular.

However, it is important to bear in mind that a
diagram such as illus. 19 represents a concept; it is
not a plan. It functions in the mind of the architect
like a mnemonic – as a shorthand depiction of the
ideas outlined above and elaborated only verbally in
the texts – it is not a blueprint. For a town to be
built in exact visual accordance with such a diagram
would only be possible if it were built in a single
process, on a previously clear site. And in reality
that never occurs. The great majority of towns and
cities in India (as elsewhere) have grown
incrementally over long periods, not from one pre-
ordained plan. The opportunities for new, planned
cities are comparatively rare, and even then no site
is wholly without features.

Moreover, in spite of this limitation, the archaeological record does in fact contain some instructive
examples, most of which are perfectly well known.
In the south of India there are a number of cities
where the sacred association of the site is crucial.
The city of Madurai, though of earlier foundation,
was redeveloped under Nayaka patronage in the

20 Sketch-plan of the city of Madurai in the 18th century (with the temple shaded).

21 Plan of the Ranganatha temple at Srirangam (after Fergusson).

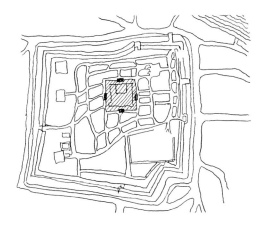

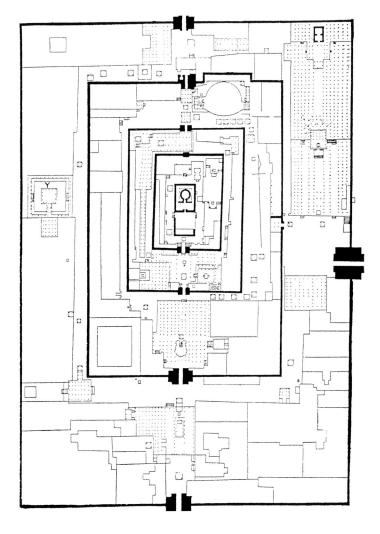

22 Representation of the Ranganatha temple at Srirangam
by an Indian artist.

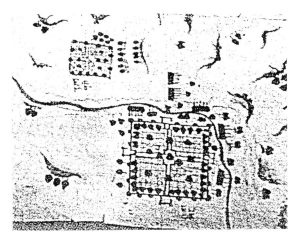

23 Representation of Sanganer, from an 18th-century painted plan in the Maharaja Sawai Man Singh II Museum, Jaipur.

seventeenth century, and is centred on the ancient shrine of Minakshi-Sundareshvara. Minakshi was born a Pandyan princess but became a goddess through her marriage with the pan-Indian god Shiva (known as Sundareshvara, the beautiful Lord). The site is therefore one that connects local royal power with the Hindu pantheon. In a similar way, Vijayanagara, the capital of the most powerful southern empire between the thirteenth century and the sixteenth, was founded on ground identified as Kishkinda, the scene of a decisive episode in the pan-Indian epic the *Ramayana*. Incidents of the story are marked on the landscape. And, as if this were not enough, here too stands the shrine of a local goddess, Pampa, who became a consort of Shiva.

The town plan of Madurai, as developed by the Nayakas, involves a grid of streets surrounding the temple, which is thereby fixed in the *brahmasthana* of a *mandala*. An even clearer example of the fulfilment of this same model is the celebrated temple-city of Srirangam (built between the thirteenth century and the eighteenth). Here we

find the optimum seven concentric enclosures, with the temple at the centre, surrounded first by its lesser shrines and offices, and further out by the houses of the citizens. The geometrical irregularities of both Madurai and Srirangam when they are rendered as modern plans (illus. 20 and 21) are something to which we shall return. For the moment we may note that if the mandalic conception of these places sometimes escapes the attention of modern archaeologists, it is nevertheless made abundantly clear by indigenous, conceptual representations of them (illus. 22).

Turning to the north of India, to find examples closer to Jaipur, there is Dabhoi, a town of thirteenth-century origin in Gujarat, and Sanganer, founded in the early eleventh century within the former state of Amber. In plan both are simpler than the paradigm as drawn in illus. 19. Each employs a 2 x 2 square *mandala*, conforming to the type defined above as a *kevala nagara*: the outer wall is pierced by four gates at the cardinal points, while the town has two bisecting roads, from north to south and from west to east, meeting at a central crossroads (illus. 23). Also following the same pattern is the late seventeenth-century town of Sikar, in the Shekhavati district, 30 miles to the north-west of Jaipur.

The realization of the shastric concept is not a matter of selective obedience to the texts, but of opportunity. The *shastras* define the conceptual model that is to hand whenever a town is planned. The precise manner in which it is rendered in any given case will naturally be influenced by other factors. Changing political and social conditions will modify how the model is perceived at a given moment, and how it is fulfilled will depend considerably on the pre-existing features of the selected site. Given the unpredictability of such fac-tors, there cannot be a uniform way of realizing the ideal. Chapter Two shows in detail how such factors affected the implementation of the concept in the case of Jaipur.

Literary Cities

An official court history of Jaipur, composed during the reign of Sawai Ram Singh II one hundred years after the foundation of the city, eulogizes its distinctive aspects, speaking of the king's palace with its golden pinnacles and battlements, the beautiful crossroads and bazaars, the numerous balconies and stone screens, and the traders and shopkeepers who sit like Kubera (the rotund god of wealth) in front of their stalls.[35] This account combines straightforward descriptions of features that are still to be seen in Jaipur today, with images drawn from the standard repertoire of Indian literature. In doing so it points to a further expression of the conceptual city, parallel to that offered by the more technical *shastras*, that had equally been available to the imaginations of those who first fashioned and inhabited Jaipur.

Here, for example, is a description of the city of Ayodhya from the *Ramayana* of Tulsidas:

> Narada and Sanaka and all the great sages came every day to Ayodhya to see the king of Kosala. The appearance of the city made them forget all their asceticism. There were balconies inlaid with gold and jewels, splendid pavements laid in diverse colours, magnificent forts on every side of the city with their brightly painted battlements, as though the nine planets had been mustered in array to beleaguer Indra's capital, Amaravati, and floors so beautifully inlaid with coloured crystal that the soul of any saint would be distracted at the sight; the glistening palaces

were so lofty that they touched the sky with pinnacles that put to shame the brightness of sun and moon, while the lattices gleamed with jewels and the jewelled lamps shone in every room . . . The elegance of the market places was beyond all description, and things could be had without price. How is it possible to sing of the riches of the city where the spouse of Laksmi [i.e., Rama, spouse of Sita-Laksmi] reigned as king? Cloth-merchants, money-changers and grain-dealers sat at their stalls like so many Kuberas. Everyone was happy, everyone well-conducted and comely, men and women, young and old, alike.[36]

The extent to which such a passage employs standard tropes may be gauged by comparing it with the account of Videha, from the same source:

> The beauty of the city was indescribable; wherever one went there was something to charm the soul. Handsome bazaars and gorgeous balconies all studded with jewels, as though the Creator had fashioned them with his own hand; thriving bankers and traders, the very Kuberas of wealth, sitting with all their various goods displayed; fine squares and beautiful streets, that were constantly sprinkled with fragrant waters; magnificent temples to all the gods, as bright as if they had been painted by Kamadeva himself; all the people of the city, both men and women, were prosperous, well-dressed, virtuous, pious, intelligent and accomplished. But Janaka's palace was such a masterpiece that the gods tired themselves with looking at it, and the mind was quite overcome by the sight of the Fort, for it seemed to have appropriated to itself all that was most beautiful in the world. With glistening white walls and doors of gold with gems set in different devices,

the exquisite mansion where Sita dwelt was far too lovely for words to describe. All the city gates were most massive with panels of adamant, and were thronged with feudatory princes and their retinue of dancers, panegyrists and bards. The vast and well-built stables were at all hours of the day crowded with horses, elephants and chariots: and the ministers, generals and warriors all had residences in the same style as the king.[37]

The cities of Ayodhya and Videha, associated especially with Rama and Sita respectively, are here mythical places, the abodes of gods. But even as Tulsidas strives to make them sound perfect, he strives equally to make them sound real. He exaggerates features that were familiar to the eyes of his late medieval audience. And just as he is inspired by reality, so in turn his universally known text conjures the image of an ideal city against which his audience can measure the real cities that they inhabit. Just as he invokes Amaravati, the capital of Indra's heaven, as a gauge to measure the splendour of Ayodhya, so he presents his literary cities as a measure for real ones. And so his accounts reveal a dimension of a pre-colonial Indian conception of what a city might aspire to be.

24 Ganesh Pol, Jaipur Palace.

2 A Time and a Place

The previous chapter described some of the more durable features of the indigenous Indian idea of a royal city. How this idea was translated into reality depended, as we have suggested, on a range of variables, including the particular historical and political circumstances, the architectural style prevailing at the time and the challenges presented by the chosen site. One illustration of how these variables conditioned the translation of the idea into reality is provided by the city of Jaipur, founded in north-eastern Rajasthan in 1727, at a time of waning Mughal authority and resurgent Rajput power. Amongst other sources, we have drawn especially on the official court histories commissioned by the successive Maharajas of Jaipur up to the end of the eighteenth century, and on a collection of early maps and plans still preserved in the palace archives.

Amber and the Mughals

The Kachchwaha rulers of Amber are best remembered for their close association with the expansion and governance of the Mughal empire. Whether they are seen as the servile dupes of an alien imperial regime, or as far-sighted princes who helped to build a new order within India, naturally depends on the view that is taken of the Mughal period more generally. The comparison is made with another prestigious Rajput clan, the Sisodias of Mewar, who attempted to sustain a more detached stance, which some construe as proudly independent, others as ruinously stubborn. Although such perceptions were undoubtedly factors in the forging of political alliances at the time, geography also played a prominent role, as the Sisodias' capital at Udaipur nestles in a fold of the southern end of the Aravalli hills, while Amber state lies in the north-east corner of Rajasthan, vulnerably close to the Mughal imperial centres of Delhi and Agra, with which its own later capital at Jaipur forms what in recent times the tourist industry has liked to call the 'Golden Triangle'.

The Kachchwahas' initial responses to Muslim presence, to be sure, were hostile. Early rulers of Amber had fought alongside the great Rajput leader Prithviraj Chauhan of Delhi against the forces of Muhammad of Ghur at the end of the twelfth century, and, in a close repetition of history, alongside Maharana Sanga of Mewar against the invading first Mughal Babur at the battle of Khanua in 1527. In both encounters the Rajput confederacy was soundly defeated, a lesson the Kachchwahas at least could not afford to overlook.

The change came in 1562. On 20 January of that year the still young Mughal Emperor Akbar, while making a pilgrimage to the Chishti shrine at Ajmer, paused at Sanganer, a major commercial town within Amber state, and was there received by the Raja of Amber, Bhar Mal.[1] For over half a millennium Bhar Mal's ancestors had ruled this region as independent kings: the Kachchwahas had migrated from Gwalior in the tenth century to establish themselves at Dhundar (from which the local dialect takes its name), and around 1150 had wrested control of Amber from Mina tribesmen, and made it their capital (illus. 4). Akbar now persuaded him to join the imperial service. The advantage to the Mughals of this treaty was to secure the route to the Emperor's present destination, the pilgrimage centre at Ajmer, and beyond to the ports of Gujarat. The advantage to Amber was the immediate return of territory recently lost to Rao Maldeo of Jodhpur, and beyond that, a privileged status within the empire.

The treaty was sealed with a marriage between a Kachchwaha princess and Akbar, creating what was to become one of many such matrimonial alliances between the Rajput clans and the Mughal imperial house. The first major beneficiary was Raja Man Singh (r. 1592–1615), the nephew of and eventual successor to Bhar Mal, who enjoyed a distinguished career as a Mughal general and governor, serving his imperial master and brother-in-law often in far-flung corners of the empire, notably in Bengal. Two generations later a similar position of trust and service was occupied by the 'Mirza' Raja, Jai Singh I (r. 1623–67), under the Emperor Shah Jahan. By this time most other Rajput rajas had similarly sought alliance and employment, challenging the pre-eminence of the Kachchwahas but also establishing wider patterns of patronage and a more general consensus (illus. 25). This arrangement brought greater stability but meant the Rajputs sometimes had to endure long absences from their home states.

Productive relations of this sort were markedly soured in the course of the long reign of Aurangzeb (1656–1707). As both Rajput leaders and at least one of the imperial princes recorded, some of the Emperor's religious policies weakened the perception of the empire as a shared enterprise.[2] Nevertheless, when Maharaja Sawai Jai Singh II came to the throne of Amber in 1699, he started out typically enough, performing early services for the Emperor in the Deccan (illus. 5). But when the death of Aurangzeb led to a war of succession between his two sons, Shah Alam and Azam Shah, Sawai Jai Singh backed the latter, who turned out to be the loser, at the battle of Jajau on 8 June 1707; and as a punishment for this tactical error, Amber was invested by Mughal troops. The dispossessed young Raja turned to other Rajput leaders for assistance, and particularly to Jodhpur, which had suffered a similar fate, and Udaipur, which had reserved its position and so was better placed to be of help. Having the whip hand in this triple alliance, and before embarking on a potentially perilous enterprise, the Maharana of Udaipur specified as a condition for his support that any son born to his allies by a Sisodia rani should be preferred for the succession in their states. As the condition was tacit rather than explicit, it was the more readily accepted, and Jodhpur was duly recovered by the three combined forces in July 1708, and Amber in the following October.[3]

Such a strike against Mughal authority could scarcely meet with acquiescence, but fortunately for the Rajputs, Shah Alam, who ruled as Bahadur Shah, died in 1712, before he could do anything to reverse it. And Sawai Jai Singh enjoyed much better relations with his successors. The short-lived Jahandar Shah (r. 1712–13) appointed him governor of Malwa, a position he maintained off and on through much of the reign of Farrukh Siyar (r. 1713–19); and he developed a particularly close understanding with Muhammad Shah (r. 1719–48). By this time, however, having the confidence of the

25 Akbari diplomacy: the Emperor receives the keys of the fort at
Gagraun from its governor in 1561; from an *Akbarnama* of *c.* 1590.

Emperor was less critical than it had once been. The rapid succession of emperors had somewhat eroded the prestige of the office. The transition from Farrukh Siyar to Muhammad Shah in 1719 had been particularly messy, with two imperial ministers, the Saiyyid brothers, acting as power brokers, and trying out, each for a few months at a time, a variety of pliable Mughal princes. Leading Rajput rajas were active participants in the Saiyyids' conspiracies, and while they thus sought to secure their own immediate interests they also contributed to a process that undermined the personal authority of the Emperor.

The sense that the Emperor was no longer the director but a tool, however essential, of the imperial machine, was to lead eventually to a lessening of the authority of the empire itself. This point was made clear in dramatic fashion by the temporary invasion and sack of Delhi by Nadir Shah of Iran in 1739, when the Emperor's treasured peacock throne and the Koh-i-Noor were looted, and he was powerless to protect the citizens of his capital from massacre. Less sudden than this catastrophe but even more damaging to Mughal power were the continuing disturbances and encroachments of the Marathas in the south, and the Sikhs in the north-west.

The City as Self-Assertion

Within this context of Mughal decline and general upheaval in the empire, Sawai Jai Singh sought to assert himself and his kingdom as an alternative power base. The founding of a new capital city in the late 1720s was merely one part of a wider policy to establish Kachchwaha pre-eminence with respect not only to the waning Mughal court but also against the other Hindu (including the other Rajput) courts. With the hindsight of history, such an observation may appear exaggerated, as

ultimately his efforts were not successful, or at least his achievements were not enduring, because the rapid rise of the Jats and the Marathas caused a turmoil in which no single power could long stand prominent. But it is worth assessing his efforts to emulate and surpass his contemporaries in the interlocking domains of politics, religion and commerce.

In addition to enhancing his personal prestige through his career in the Mughal administration, Sawai Jai Singh was active in domestic politics, restructuring Amber into divisions or *nizamats* to create a modern state with a feudal hierarchy, parallel to that of the Mughals.[4] The reorganization of the royal household into specialist departments or *karkhanas* was again modelled on that of the Mughals, though it employed vernacular terms and the ideal Hindu number 36, as later described in the *Buddhi Vilas* of Bakhta Rama Shah Chaksu.[5] The founding of a new capital city, named after himself, was the most visible outward sign of this reordering of the state.

Also of significance here is the matter of the curious title 'Sawai', which literally means 'one and a quarter'. The story of its origin involves a meeting with Aurangzeb in 1696, when Jai Singh was still a young prince. When the ageing Emperor reportedly took the boy by the hand and asked if he had any reason to fear him, Jai Singh replied that, as a groom takes his bride by the hand as a sign of his protection, he could fear nothing from a master who has made the same gesture. Impressed by this presence of mind, Aurangzeb commented that the boy surpassed his illustrious forebear and namesake the great Jai Singh I, who had been known as the Mirza Raja (an epithet that implies learning), indeed that he surpassed most men: he was *sawai*. Later Jai Singh sought to use this casual compliment as a title. But all such titles had to be conferred by the Mughal court and it was not until 1713 (unsurprisingly after the death of his enemy Bahadur Shah) that he gained the necessary sanction.[6] That he pestered for it for so long indicates its symbolic significance, marking him as unique amongst the Rajput rajas.

In the realm of religion too, Sawai Jai Singh sought to project himself as surpassing other rulers. Personally, he was in his youth a devotee of the god Rama, but in adulthood he became a major patron of the worship of Krishna, engaging in debate with the leading *goswamis* (learned priests) at Vrindavan and commissioning explanatory and devotional texts from them. This interest was directly connected to his management of his state, through the installation in Jaipur of the image of Shri Govind (illus. 6), which was originally housed in Vrindavan in the temple especially commissioned by his ancestor Raja Man Singh I (illus. 26). Together with the construction of temples in Jaipur this kind of activity would have been perceived as a fulfilment of the normal duties of a Hindu king.

But Sawai Jai Singh audaciously exceeded those normal expectations through the public performance of two particular Vedic rituals. The Vajapeya Yajna was performed in 1708, and was described in a specially commissioned text, the *Ramavilasa Kavyam* of Vishvanatha Ranade, as well as in the official history of his reign, the *Sawai Jai Singh Charit* of Kavi Atmaram, and in that of his successor. As these texts remind us, this rite is associated exclusively with a universal ruler, a king of the highest order; indeed that 'he obtained the

26 The entrance to the Govind Dev temple at Vrindavan.

title of Samrat (emperor) by performing the Vajapeya'.[7] It should not escape our notice that Sawai Jai Singh commissioned the performance of this highly charged rite at a time when he had only just recovered his grip on the reigns of power, as if to declare his self-confidence in the aftermath of the Mughal occupation. Much later in his reign he twice commissioned another Vedic ritual, the Ashvamedha Yajna, which similarly may be performed only by paramount kings.[8] In these actions, Sawai Jai Singh was going far beyond what was considered normal – or even acceptable – amongst his peers. He was publicly declaring his rights as a paramount sovereign, and commemorating and advertising the claim in texts. More generally, throughout his reign he set himself up personally as an arbiter of religious disputes, receiving missions from as far afield as Bengal,[9] and in this he was perhaps being even more audacious, since such arbitration was not normally a function of even the greatest of kings.

Alongside such activities it was important for Sawai Jai Singh to identify his state not only as a political and sacred centre but also as a commercial one. This aspect of his ambition was especially integral to the establishment of a new capital, which from the outset was conceived as a leading trading city. Geography was on his side, as the state lay between the centres of imperial power to the east and the ports of the west coast. But Sawai Jai Singh did not leave it to geography alone. The *Buddhi Vilas* mentions that he sent personal invitations to noted merchants of the time, offering them tax concessions and gifts of land on which to build houses, if they agreed to settle in Jaipur.[10] Jain merchants especially were targeted, to ensure that the city became a centre of banking and high-capital industries such as gem trading (which indeed Jaipur remains today).

A more forceful inducement was offered to the *thakurs*, the chiefs of the state's divisions: a *haveli* (residence) was built for each within the city, but the cost was recovered through the remission to the state of 10 per cent of their incomes, effectively obliging them to establish their own headquarters within the capital.[11] This device enhanced the new city's political prestige, and it also had some equally desirable side-effects. By distributing the chiefs around the city, Sawai Jai Singh ensured that a wealthy dignitary had a personal interest in the maintenance of services in each of its districts. By obliging the *thakurs* to attend in the capital, he also kept them by his side, thus limiting the extent to which they could build autonomous power within their *thikanas* (domains) – a reflection of the policy adopted by the Mughals with respect to the Maharajas themselves. And of course their presence in Jaipur created a market for the luxury goods in which the merchants traded.

For the commercial dimension to his policy, the increasing turbulence of the eighteenth century worked to Sawai Jai Singh's advantage. Sikh depredations in the Punjab especially merely promoted the reputation of Jaipur as a safe haven for traders. Contemporary texts such as the *Bhojansara* of Girdhari (1739) attest to the city's instant commercial success.[12] Other documents reveal a carefully planned two-part strategy. In the early years Jaipur was guaranteed a role as an entrepôt of high-quality goods from the Mughal cities and from the rich trading towns of Gujarat, as the Jaipur merchants had to undertake to trade in such commodities within Jaipur alone. By 1742, when the city's success was firmly established, this policy was thrown into reverse and the market was protected, as the merchants had to agree to trade only in the produce of the Jaipur state.[13]

The Site

Five miles to the south of Amber lies an open plain bounded on the north-west and the east by hills. This was the site that Sawai Jai Singh selected for his new capital. Earlier Rajput capitals were established amongst hills – Amber itself is a prime example, with its naturally defended location in a gorge – and the move onto a plain is a measure of Sawai Jai Singh's boldness. The choice of site was also an indication of the changing conception of the capital, from a military retreat cut off from invading forces to a trading centre open to good communications. Even so, the change was not extreme and the hills afforded some welcome protection. Those to the north-west are part of a continuous ridge linking the site to Amber and thus providing fortifiable communication between the new city and the old. The latter, with its protective fort of Jaigarh, remained the place of final retreat.

Besides the hills there are certain other pre-existing features of this site that were to play a role in shaping the city (illus. 27). The plain had previously been used as a hunting ground and near the north-western corner Sawai Jai Singh had in 1713 built a pleasure garden with a hunting lodge, known as Jai Niwas, and a small lake called Tal Katora.[14] This establishment was not to be sacrificed: according to Girdhari's *Bhojansara* of 1739, Sawai Jai Singh specified that 'Jai Niwas should come within this city, this is my wish'.[15] Here, then, was one feature the new city had to accommodate.

Another feature was a road traversing the plain from north to south, linking Amber, the capital, with Sanganer, which at the time was the state's principal trading town. This road had to be preserved and controlled and therefore had to fall within the city's boundaries. A second road traversed the plain from east to west. This one formed part of the road between the Mughal cities of Agra and Ajmer, making proximity again desirable, since to place the new city on an already established communication line would help to secure its economic success. But in this case it was an imperial road and could not be encroached upon. The city therefore had to be contained within the northern end of the plain, to the north of this line. At the far northern end of the plain a large marshy area marked the northernmost limit.

A further decisive natural feature is that the plain is not quite flat. A long and straight ridge runs across the plain, parallel to the Agra–Ajmer road and some distance to the north of it, again in a roughly west–east alignment (the line in fact deviates 15° from the cardinal axes). The area to the south of this ridge is even, while that to the north slopes gently downwards. The ridge is still plainly visible on the ground today. In shastric terms the arrangement is ideal, as a declivity towards the north-east is considered the best possible kind of site. In practical terms, the ridge too had to be accommodated.

Finally, in the hills to the east of the plain is a sacred site known as Galtaji. This had been a retreat for ascetics since the early sixteenth century and at this time was the centre of the Ramanandis, a Vaishnavite sect.[16] Although the new city was to be restricted to the plain, Galtaji was a crucial element in the pre-existing sacred geography of the site.

USING THE DESIGN CONCEPT

Bearing in mind the conceptual city or shastric paradigm, and the features of the chosen site, the layout of the city of Jaipur resolves itself. The design process entails developing the site in the light of the paradigm, and this calculation can readily be reconstructed. First, there was the

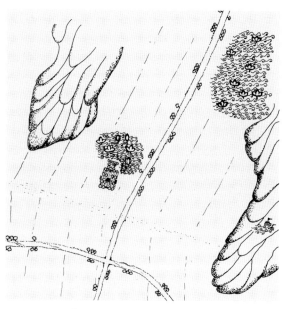

27 Conjectural reconstruction of the site for Jaipur.

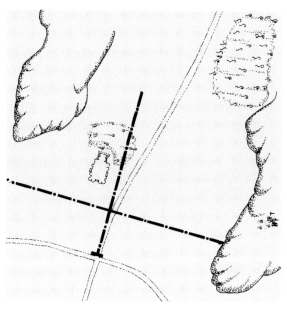

28 Establishing the city's axes on the site.

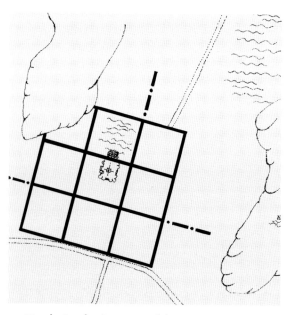

29 Developing the site as a *mandala*.

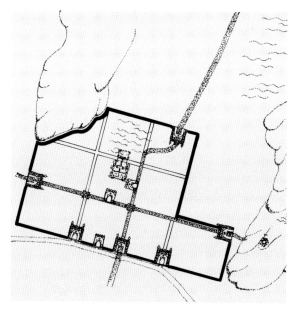

30 Accommodating the western and eastern adjustments.

immutable natural feature of the ridge. Although not perfectly aligned with the east–west axis, this straight line suggested itself as the route for one of the main east–west thoroughfares. Building a road along the crest of a ridge makes best use of the topography for the purposes of drainage, while, by contrast, ignoring the ridge and building a road obliquely across it would not only fail to capitalize on this given advantage but would also create an awkward kink at the point of crossing.

With this first line established as one of the east–west routes, what followed was to regularize the Amber–Sanganer road as a north–south route at right angles to it (illus. 28). The point of intersection would therefore be one of the city's crossroads (*chaupar*). To the north-west of this intersection lay the garden and hunting lodge. Given that Jai Niwas was to be included at the express command of the patron, and given that its royal association meant that it had to be within the palace compound, the site of the palace was established. Indeed, given the wish to locate the palace centrally, the position of the *brahmasthana* was also established. The roads described thus became its southern and eastern boundaries, and the crossing its south-east corner.

But although the general location and the axes of two sides of the *brahmasthana* were thus determined, its precise dimensions were not. The positions of two sides were given, but their length (and thus the position of the other two sides of the square) depended on something else. The southern boundary of the city had to lie within the line of the Agra–Ajmer road, running roughly parallel to the ridge to the south. Extending the north-south road as far as possible southwards beyond the crossing up to the imperial road established the distance between the crossing and a city gate. This gives the first fixed dimension, the length of the side of a square, and so establishes the size of the unit or module of the city. Filling in the squares of the *mandala* could now proceed (illus. 29).

An apparent problem arose in the north-west corner, where there was insufficient space to complete the *mandala* because of the intrusion of the hill. Although in shastric terms a diminution of the site in the north-west is far from ideal, in one practical respect this unavoidable arrangement was actually an advantage: the contiguity of the city to the hill enhanced its security by preventing the possibility of a force coming between them. And indeed this proximity was exploited to the full. On the summit of the ridge above the city, Sawai Jai Singh had constructed a fort known as Nahargarh or Sudarshangarh, as a place of retreat. Walls extending over the whole range of hills connected this fort with Jaigarh, the fort above the old capital at Amber. Jaigarh contains the gun foundry, and was also remodelled at this time.[17] So at the time of building the new city a whole network of fortifications was created, in which the north-west hill played a key role.

The profile of the hill also explains why the western sectors or squares of the city are slightly wider than the others. To maximize the protection afforded by the hill, the point of contact between it and the city's western wall was made at the hill's southern apex, and this established a western boundary some distance to the west of where mathematical purity would have placed it (illus. 30).

If it was necessary and strategic to restrict the city on the north-west corner, it also proved advantageous to extend it on the opposite corner, in the south-east, by the addition of an extra square. The extension of a given direction is a normal procedure and represents no violation of the planning principles – indeed, extensions towards the north and east are recommended by the texts. In

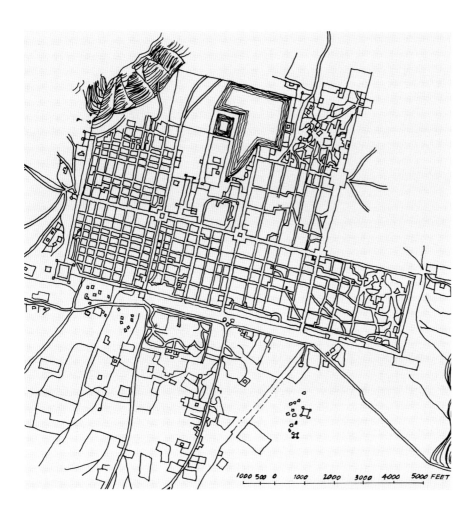

1000 500 0   1000   2000   3000   4000   5000 FEET

this particular case, the extension achieved a number of further advantages. First, it plugged the gap between the city and the eastern hills, thus again closing access to any invading force and especially protecting the route towards Amber. Second, it allowed the main east–west road within the city to extend towards Galta, thus linking the sacred site into the city scheme. Third, it maximized the southern front of the city (that is, the front visible along the imperial road), thus enhancing the city's apparent scale and prestige. Fourth, and perhaps most importantly, it placed the gate on the Sanganer road (now known as Sanganeri Gate) at the centre

point of the southern wall. The gate protects the main north–south thoroughfare, the primary axis of movement within the city. The *brahmasthana* or centre of the *mandala* is occupied by the palace, but by definition this zone cannot be a thoroughfare. Following shastric convention, the palace complex faces east in the sense that its entrance gate opens onto this road on its eastern boundary. The road is therefore also the route to and from the palace, and it is appropriate that the gate that marks its end should stand centrally in the city wall. This last function also accounts for the dimension of the eastern extension: to ensure the centrality of the

Sanganeri Gate, it has to match the extra width of the western wards.

A comparison of the shastric diagram with the evolved plan (illus. 19 and 30) shows clearly both the continuity of the concept and the modifications required by the exigencies of the site. It would be a mistake to regard these modifications as imperfections or errors. The translation of the paradigm into a reality is a process that inevitably entails managing a real site, and the authors of *vastu shastra* knew this. What matters is sustaining the concept – the mental model – and the plan of Jaipur achieves this. When walking through the streets of Jaipur one is acutely and constantly aware of its layout, of the broad straight streets arranged on a grid with the palace centrally placed; and it is this mental experience – not the visual inspection of a modern map (illus. 31) – that makes us recognize the *mandala*. To superimpose the shastric *mandala* back over a map of Jaipur and to mark the discrepancies would be to the miss the point. The city as built is a successful rendering of the *mandala* concept because it looks and feels like a *mandala* when one is in it.

This point is worth pursuing in relation to one prominent modification. The streets, as described, are not aligned with the points of the compass, but run along an axis of 15° to accommodate the ridge. However, this is not observable on the ground. The precise positions of the rising and the setting of the sun vary through the year, but they are never far off the axis of the main east–west street running across the city. To reinforce the association, the gates marking the western and eastern ends of this street are respectively named Chand Pol (moon gate) and Suraj Pol (sun gate). Furthermore, by a freak of nature the ridge on the plain is aligned with a small but marked peak in the eastern hills

by Galta. On a platform on this peak, Sawai Jai Singh constructed a Surya temple. Surya, the sun god, is of course associated with the east. He is also the ancestor both of Rama, the god worshipped by the ascetics of Galta, and of the ruling house of Jaipur. This temple is plainly visible through the entire length of the main west–east street of the city, being perfectly aligned with its axis. Whatever a compass may say, the experience is of an alignment. The street runs to the east because it points to Surya. Thus the orientation of the city is woven at once into the sacred geography and the natural topography of the site.

SOME MISCONCEPTIONS ABOUT THE PLAN OF JAIPUR

The recognition of the shastric basis of the planning of Jaipur establishes an important point about *vastu vidya* in general – namely that it is a mental, not a graphic, tool. The test, favoured by some scholars,[18] of drawing *mandalas* over a measured plan of a building or a city – whether intended to demonstrate correspondence or discrepancy – is fundamentally mistaken. In the first place, it is unhistorical. Invoking measured scale drawings as a test introduces a comparison that the architects themselves could not have made, since the use of such drawings was not a usual part of architectural practice in pre-colonial India. In post-Renaissance Western architectural history, it is reasonable to compare ideal conceptions with measured drawings that we ourselves have prepared, because we can fairly assume some correspondence between our drawings and those that were made at the time: we assume that they too visualized and depicted their designs in such terms. In the Indian historical context this assumption would be false. There, typically, the ideal was realized in built form on the site (in the manner just described in the case of Jaipur) without the intermediary stage of the scale drawing. This explains why, although some contemporary maps and other depictions of Jaipur have survived, no scale design drawings exist. What matters is a correspondence not between a shastric diagram and a measured plan, but between a shastric paradigm (carried mentally) and an experience on the ground.

Measured plans of Madurai, Srirangam and the other examples mentioned in Chapter One similarly reveal what are sometimes taken to be imperfections. Not all the streets are perfectly straight, not all the intersections are perfect right angles, and so on. But again, these geometrical irregularities can be explained in relation to the features of the site. They are much less apparent on the ground than on a plan, and they do not diminish the correspondence between one's perception of the form and the mental paradigm. As one penetrates the temple of Srirangam, for example, one is most conscious of the concentric enclosures and the sequence of gates, and without pausing to measure all the alignments, one grasps that one is within a *mandala*. Our experience of such places is often more faithfully represented by indigenous depictions (illus. 22), and this of course is their purpose: they record our understanding of the site.

The modifications of the model that were required in the case of Jaipur, and the 'match and test' approach to *vastu vidya*, have led some – including even the city's leading historian, A. K. Roy – to dismiss the shastric basis of Jaipur's plan altogether.[19] One writer explicitly rules out any such inspiration precisely on the ground that a regular *mandala* cannot be superimposed over a measured plan and urges that the approach was instead 'based first and foremost upon practical considerations'.[20] To say that practice is practical is to state the obvious. But complex practices are underpinned by theory. To fail to see the role of shastric theory underlying the design is like asserting that a piece of music ignores the conventions of composition, or that a speech ignores grammar, simply because the rules cannot be heard. If we superimpose Panini's grammar over Valmiki's *Ramayana* we will find that the texts are not the same; should we conclude that the epic is not in Sanskrit?

Aside from the view that the plan of Jaipur is not shastric, it is sometimes asserted that before Jaipur there was no practice of town planning in India, especially in the north, and that Jaipur therefore represents a first.[21] But the examples already given above show that this is an overstatement. What is true is that towns planned on a previously clear site and built rapidly are comparatively rare, since the majority of Indian towns evolve gradually. Most of the earlier Rajput capitals, in addition, were built on hilly sites where a regular grid could not be imposed. Even here, though, there is a topological system: the centrality of the fortified palace, the fortified city wall with gates on all sides, and the attachment of the centre to the periphery by means of the main street, are all common principles of the earlier Rajput capitals.[22] What is unusual (though not unique) about Jaipur is the implementation of this same pattern as an orthogonal grid.

A third recurrent confusion amongst writers on Jaipur's plan relates to the identification of the precise shastric model that was adopted from the many available. Some of those writers who agree that there was such a model take the *prastara* as the key. This idea was first advanced by E. B. Havell, who thought he detected similarities between the

32 The *prastara* plan, as drawn by Ram Raz (1834).

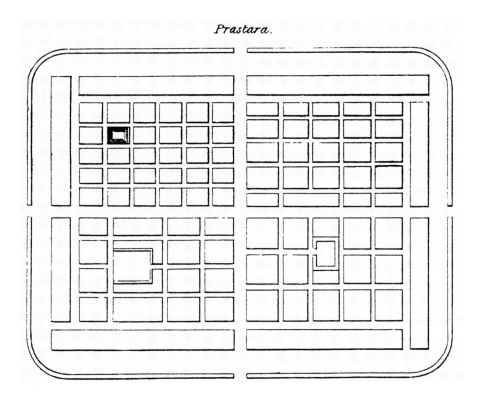

Prastara.

plan of Jaipur and the *prastara* as drawn by Ram Raz in an early study of the *Manasara*, and the identification has been accepted by others.[23] It is not sustainable. Ram Raz's drawing was itself conjectural and bears little relation to the form described by the text he purported to illustrate (illus. 32).[24] And Jaipur itself bears little relation either to his drawing or to the textual original: the only common element is the grid, which is of course common to all of the town plan types offered by the texts. The *prastara* in this context is a complex type of plan developed from the mandalic base.[25] It is that mandalic base itself that the planners of Jaipur employed, preferring those versions in the sequence of *mandalas* with the unit three – that is, having a multiple of three squares to each side. In its simplest form, this is a 3 x 3 square grid called *pitha*; but it also includes the more

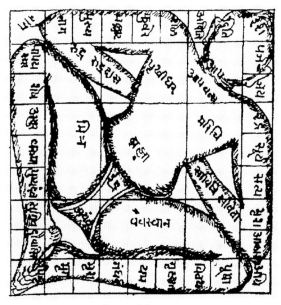

33 Base 3 *vastu purusha mandala*.

45

commonly used *paramashayika*, with nine squares to each side (illus. 2 and 33). In practice these two versions of the *mandala* are interchangeable, the latter being a more complex version of the former. They are to be distinguished from versions that employ the number two as a base (for example, the 8 x 8 square *chandita*). The main difference with regard to town planning is that an even-sided *mandala* produces a crossroads in the centre, while an odd-sided one delivers the desired central square.

A fourth misconception is the idea that the regularity of Jaipur's plan is an indication of European influence.[26] It is true that Sawai Jai Singh's activities in the field of astronomy were informed to a limited extent by Western science; and certainly as a patron he was open to foreign ideas. But Jaipur's contact with Europe historically came after the establishment of the city.[27] More importantly, external influence is not necessary since the plan can be wholly explained within the indigenous system. It is perhaps tempting for European writers to see Western influence everywhere, and the attribution of Jaipur's plan to a Western source is reminiscent of the once fashionable attribution of the Taj Mahal to Italian jewellers.

There is also confusion about the authorship of the plan. The sentimental school of art history often seeks to attribute great designs to the patron, and Jaipur is no exception, with some writers handing the palm to Sawai Jai Singh himself.[28] This latter-day court flattery is an irrelevance. A more intriguing figure is Vidyadhar, identified as the architect both in the popular imagination and by some authorities.

Vidyadhar was descended from one Ratnagarbha Sarvabhauma Bhattacharya, a Bengali *pandit* (priest) who came to Amber with the image of Shila Devi installed in the Amber fort. Vidyadhar was the grandson of the priest's daughter, his own patronymic being Chakravarty. He is mentioned in some contemporary texts, including Girdhari's *Bhojansara* and Krishna Bhatta's *Ishvarvilas Mahakavyam*. These sources show that plans for private houses – for example, those of merchants who had been invited to settle in Jaipur – had to be approved by Vidyadhar in order to maintain state control and ensure uniformity in heights and building types. A letter from Sawai Jai Singh to one such merchant, Ghasiram Murlidhar, tells him to 'act according to the instructions of Vidyadhar'. Vidyadhar was also responsible for overseeing the remission of 10 per cent of the *thakurs'* income to cover the costs of their houses in the city. More generally, the *Bhojansara* says that 'Sawai laid the foundation of Jaipur . . . He said to Vidyadhara that a city should be founded here'; and the *Ishvarvilas Mahakavyam* recalls that 'the famous Rajadhiraj Sawai Jai Singh founded the beautiful city of Jaipur by dint of his [Vidyadhar's] wisdom and knowledge'.[29]

These passages have been used to support the attribution of the design variously to Sawai Jai Singh and to Vidyadhar. But they imply neither. In the light of what else we know of these figures, the texts describe nothing more than a patron giving instructions to a minister. There is no mention of the character of the design, nor even of the act of designing, which would naturally require architects skilled in *vastu vidya*. Clearly, Vidyadhar was closely involved in supervising the construction of the city, and he is associated with specific architectural projects including the City Palace and Jaigarh, but he was involved as an official of the patron, not as the designer.[30] Moreover, Vidyadhar was responsible for the education of the king's son and heir, Ishvari Singh, scarcely a role for the court architect.[31] Vidyadhar was a political figure; and indeed by 1729 he was to rise to become *desh ko diwan* (chief minister).[32] The real architects and planners of this remarkable city remain sadly unknown, as their names were probably never recorded.

Building the City

The foundation ceremony was held on V. S. Pausha Badi 1, 1784, corresponding to 29 November 1727. The same motives that led Sawai Jai Singh to establish the city encouraged also a rapid construction, and this was facilitated by the use of rubble as the principal building material. The main wards of the city had been laid out by 1734, within seven years of the foundation. In the previous year the city had been officially recognized as the state capital by the Mughal Emperor Muhammad Shah. A document known as the *Sivaha Hazuri* is a register of the daily activities of the Maharaja; the entry for Chaitra Vadi 4, 1790 (February 1734) describes Sawai Jai Singh playing Holi throughout the central parts of the city.[33] A map painted on cloth also made at about this time is evidently a progress report on the construction; it shows the location of the palace and the four central, southern and western wards (illus. 34).[34] It would be a mistake to infer from this map that originally only four wards were intended: it is plainly a record of work completed rather than a design plan.[35] We may infer rather that the city was built from west to east and from south to north, in accordance with shastric procedure, and in response to the main constraints of the site, namely the hill to the west, the road to the south and the slope towards the north. Two other eighteenth-century maps in the palace collection show the city more complete, but the northern side (and especially the north-east corner), less fully resolved than the rest

of the city, again suggesting that this area was built last (illus. 7).[36] Originally the larger size of the Tal Katora hampered the development of the northern zones, and indeed the grid of minor streets was never properly established in the north-east.

The main skeletal components of the city, built swiftly under royal patronage, include the city wall and its gates, the main streets dividing the area into wards (*chowkri*) and crossroads (*chaupar*), the palace compound wall in the centre, the façades of the shops on the main bazaars, and the principal temples. All of these components work together in an integrated system, but we shall consider each of them individually, starting from the outer boundary.

THE WALL AND GATES

The eventual outer form defined by the city wall is as shown in illus. 30. The variation between this and the originating *mandala* paradigm, as already explained, should not be seen as an abandonment or alteration of the shastric base, but as its implementation. For example, the extension of the city eastwards to meet the Galta hills and so to block the route to the north, is itself a fulfilment of the reiterated shastric idea that a city must be especially impregnable on its northern and eastern sides (illus. 8).[37]

The wall is on average 6 m high and 3 m thick. It is pierced by a total of seven gates, a shastric model number. For a temple composed of concentric zones, the ideal has seven enclosures, each with a gate on each side, thus producing four series of seven gates. This is the ideal realized at Srirangam, and frequently depicted in paintings of palaces of the gods (including one exhibited in the Jaipur palace). In the case of a city, the number is interpreted as gates around the periphery of the outer enclosure.

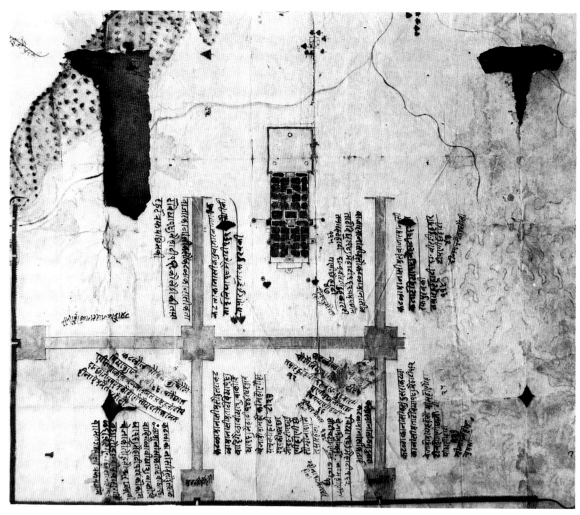

34 The 'progress report' plan, painted on cloth.

The Chand Pol on the west side and the Suraj Pol on the east mark the ends of the main west–east route through the city, about 3 km in length. On the north side, protecting the road to Amber, is the gate now called Jorawar Singh Pol, formerly named Dhruv Pol after the pole star. At intervals along the southern front are four gates. From west to east these are the Ajmeri Gate (commanding the westerly road towards Ajmer), the Naya Pol (or New Gate), the Sanganeri Gate (governing the route southwards towards that major town; illus. 9) and the Ghat Darwaza (linking the city with the easterly road towards Ghoomi Ghat, the pass through the eastern hills). This southern side, the vulnerable face that the city presented to the outer world, was originally further protected by a ditch immediately in front of the wall; this was substantially filled in during the 1950s (though one part near the Naya Pol remains).[38] All of the gates were closed at night, a practice continued until 1942.[39]

THE CHOWKRIS

The principal streets of the city define the grid of the *mandala* and divide the city into *chowkris* (wards). The names by which these are known may not be original but they do indicate some original features (illus. 35). The south-west ward and the eastern extension, for example, are known respectively as Topkhana Desh and Topkhana Hazuri (meaning 'arms store'), implying that they were conceived as the city's corner bastions. The south-east ward is Ghat Darwaza, named after its gate.

The central ward in front of the palace is divided into two halves: Modi to the west and Vishveshvarji to the east (the latter is named after a temple added in the nineteenth century).[40] The divider between these two halves is a road, Chaura Rasta, equal in width to the other main roads, and an addition to the grid. This road links the Tripolia Gate, the southern entrance to the palace compound, with the city wall and the Naya Pol, and so it emphasizes the axis of the city and the centrality of the palace, and it provides access to the palace from the south. It has been suggested that this road and the Naya Pol were afterthoughts, added in the nineteenth century.[41] Although seemingly supported by the gate's name, this idea is mistaken: both the road and the gate feature prominently in eighteenth-century representations of the city;[42] and the road's functions with respect to axis and access also plainly meet original requirements. The confusion arises because the Naya Pol was later rebuilt (and so renamed); and it is also true that some prominent buildings now lining Chaura Rasta are later structures.

The central zone of the city has three wards. From west to east these are: Purani Basti (the 'old quarter', perhaps named in remembrance of its having been the first constructed), the palace *sarahad* in

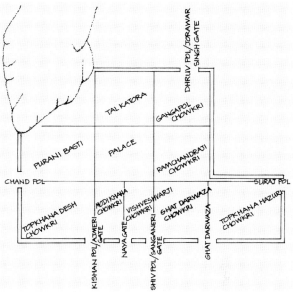

35 Sketch-plan of Jaipur indicating the wards and gates.

the centre, and Ramchandraji (named after a nineteenth-century temple; see Chapter Three). In the northern zone, the western ward is obliterated by the hill; the central ward behind the palace is filled by the Tal Katora; and the eastern side has the *chowkri* known as Gangapol, after a minor gate in the north-east corner of the city.

MOHALLAS

Just as the main roads of the grid separate the wards, so smaller grids of narrower roads subdivide them further. Some sources suggest that the main roads are all precisely 111 feet (*c.* 37 m) wide, the secondary roads exactly half that figure, and the tertiary roads a quarter width. Evidently some such system was intended, although as A. K. Roy has pointed out it was not executed with mathematical precision.[43] The main streets are all around 100 feet (*c.* 33 m) wide.

This division of the city into wards and their subdivision into sub-wards, by different scales of grid, is more than a matter of mobility and geometry. It relates to the system of social distribution, the pattern of settlement of people according to caste or *jati*, that is defined by the *shastras*, and is now more commonly known as the *mohalla* system.

The smallest social unit architecturally is the *haveli*, a courtyard house, which accommodated all the members of an extended family, and certain of their servants (illus. 10). A group or cluster of *havelis* constitutes a *mohalla*, a wider social group, tied not necessarily by blood and marriage, but by *jati*. The members of a *mohalla* form a community with professional and social bonds. Spatially the *mohalla* functions as a cell within the city, capable at times of discouraging – even prohibiting – the entry of non-members, in order to preserve the privacy of the group. The *mohallas* are separated from each other by the smaller roads, but aggregate to form a *chowkri*.

Shastric texts define the appropriate regional distribution of castes in considerable detail. Given the social upheavals of the twentieth century, it is hard at this distance of time to determine how precisely the ideal pattern was implemented. The existence of Brahmapuri, a Brahmins' quarter, outside the city wall, suggests some flexibility at least; although it is located in the north, the direction conventionally reserved for Brahmins. It is clear that the principle of social distribution by *jati* was applied, and traces of it remain today. For example, Johari Bazaar remains, as its name implies, the market for costly goods such as jewellery and fine cloth. The local tie-and-dye cloth is sold especially in Kishanpol Bazaar, and studded lac resin bangles in Maniharon ka Rasta. The sculptors of *murtis* (images of deities) still live and work in Khajanewalon ka Rasta in the western part of the city. Dealers in ground spices are to be found in Jhalaniyon ka Rasta off Kishanpol Bazaar, metalworkers in Thatheron ka Rasta off Chaura Rasta, and sellers of kitchen utensils in Tripolia Bazaar. Thirty years ago, Andreas Volwahsen observed similar clusterings of bricklayers, carpenters and basket-weavers.[44] And we know that Ramchandraji Chowkri, to the east of the palace (a direction that most shastric texts reserve for Kshatriyas), originally contained the houses of those who held official posts in the palace, and ministers of state.[45]

SHOPS IN THE PINK CITY

The shops that line the main streets of the city, and from which some of the trades described above operated, were constructed by the state to a uniform design (illus. 36). The main streets here include the long west–east street with Tripolia Bazaar as its central section, Kishanpol Bazaar running north–south on the western side of the city, its counterpart on the east side comprising both Sireh Deori Bazaar and Johari Bazaar, and Chaura Rasta in the centre. These are the streets leading to and bordering the palace *sarahad*, and so the arrangement fully accords with the shastric convention that shops should be located on the main roads and be connected with the palace of the king.[46]

The particular design of the shops is based on a type that had been well known in Rajasthan for a long time (there survive remnants of a prototype in fifteenth-century Chitor), but it includes an interesting innovation. In front of each row of shops runs a continuous open veranda, enabling shoppers to pass along in a sheltered space. (In the late twentieth century the section of veranda before each and every shop was enclosed, appropriated by

36 Shops bordering a principal bazaar.

the shopkeeper to maximize the shop space, but the original scheme was restored in 2000.[47]) On the upper storey the building line was kept back so that the roof of the veranda was clear and could serve as an upper circulation space, accessed by periodic flights of steps from the street level. This upper space could also function as a viewing platform for royal or sacred processions taking place in the streets. Here, too, recent illegal construction has disrupted the original design, though sections of the terrace survive and continue to be used in the traditional manner. The plots behind these shops were developed by private enterprise, though centrally regulated by Vidyadhar.

A further aspect of the uniformity of the shops is the pink wash on their façades. This feature is shared by the city wall and gives Jaipur its tourist industry sobriquet the Pink City. One of the most prevalent myths about Jaipur is that this colour wash was not original, and it is repeatedly suggested that it was introduced in the late nineteenth century by Maharaja Sawai Ram Singh II.[48] As we shall see in Chapter Four, it is true that Sawai Ram Singh developed the fabric and institutions of the city in interesting ways. It is also the case that his less inspired enterprises included an experiment in 1868 that involved painting every street with a different coloured wash. As soon as this was recognized as a hideous mistake, in 1870, the pink wash was restored;[49] but this royal intervention has often since been interpreted as instigating rather than restoring a tradition.[50] One version of the myth has it that the city was painted pink to celebrate the visit of the Prince of Wales in 1876. This is a confusion, based on the regular practice of giving the major public buildings a fresh coat of colour wash before the visits of distinguished people: the late nineteenth-century reports of the state's building departments record this being done on a number of occasions when Jaipur was visited by the Viceroy or similar dignitary.[51] Today planning regulations ensure the maintenance of the pink façades but leave it to individuals to determine the precise shade, and many have opted for an icing sugar hue that is far from the original terracotta (or *geru*). The latter was sustained into Ram Singh's time, and patches of it still survive on parts of the city walls.

That the *geru* wash was original is self-evident if considered in the context of the city's foundation. To reduce the time and the cost of construction, all the major buildings are made not of dressed stone but of rubble, which had to be rendered and painted. *Geru* imitates the colour of the region's sandstone, also used most notably in the Mughal imperial cities of Delhi, Agra and Fatehpur Sikri. Given that part of Sawai Jai Singh's intention was to establish his capital as an alternative power base to Mughal authority, it is not surprising that aspects of the design reflect this ambition. The design of the city wall especially echoes that of the great Mughal forts, and the colour wash completes the illusion (illus. 11). The point of the 'pink' is to look imperial. Contemporary sources bear this out: some mid-eighteenth-century paintings depicting the area around the *chougan* show terracotta buildings, and in all the maps preserved in the palace collection the walls are marked in terracotta paint.[52]

The stone used for the rubble base is the local quartzite, quarried from the hills surrounding the city. This is very mixed in colour, but ironically some of it has a pinkish hue (giving rise to the wrong but intriguing observation in popular guidebooks that Jaipur owes its colour to the use of pink sandstone). Jaipur state did not contain good stone quarries, as the best quarries for both sandstone and marble lie in regions that were then controlled by Jodhpur, with the result that these materials could be used only sparingly.[53] The use of

37 Sketch-plan showing the relationship of the palace to the principal original temples.

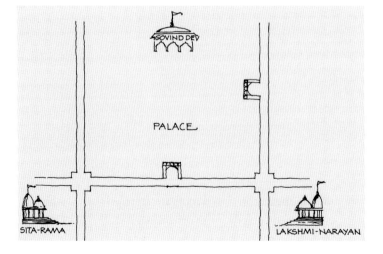

rubble from the immediately adjacent hills at least facilitated the building process by reducing transportation costs, but it also necessitated the application of a cosmetic plaster.

TEMPLES AS CITY STRUCTURE

An aspect of the city's design not widely noted is the degree to which it is structured by some of the prominent temples built at the time of foundation. Mention has already been made of the Surya temple at Galta (illus. 12), built on a peak of the eastern hills in line with the ridge carrying the city's main west–east street, and which thus helps to lock the city into the landscape. This temple was completed in 1734.[54] The dedication to Surya relates to the Maharaja's mythical descent from the Sun, through the god–king Rama. An annual event celebrating this descent linked the Surya temple to the city both ritually and spatially. Each year at the spring festival, Vasant Panchami, the image of Surya was taken out of the temple and carried through the city in a chariot attended by the Maharaja and his nobles. A witness to what must have been one of the last enactments of this ritual records the scene:

> The effigy rides in a chariot drawn by eight milk-white horses, attended by elephants with velvet hangings and gilded howdahs, camels with silken saddles and elaborate pendants, Marwari horses with flowing manes, prancing on their hind legs, and men in chain mail and helmets, armed with battle axes and long lances. The whole city joins in the universal rejoicing at the return of Spring; the streets are packed with men in long flowered gowns and many-coloured turbans, the balconies and roofs are crowded with women . . . laden with ornaments and dressed in all the colours of the rainbow . . .[55]

At strategic points within the city are two further temples. The Tripolia Bazaar, which marks the southern boundary of the palace sarahad, terminates at either end in a broad open crossroads or *chaupar*, where it meets the principal north–south bazaars. In the outer corners of these *chaupars* rise two temples. In all important respects they are a pair. Both are Vaishnavite, and both were built at the time of Jaipur's foundation, to identical designs – the characteristic *nagara* style, which was consciously archaic at the time. Each stands in a similar spatial relationship to the palace (illus. 37). The temple in the western square is the Rama Mandir, dedicated to the god–king and his consort Sita (illus. 38). The image chamber faces eastwards, towards the palace and Galtaji, that is, towards the Maharaja and their common ancestor Surya. The temple in the eastern square is dedicated to Vishnu as Lakshmi Narayan, the consort of the goddess of wealth. The image chamber faces west, towards the palace and to Johari Bazaar, the market of the wealthy traders. Thus is declared the presence at the heart of the city of the god Vishnu, with both regal and mercantile associations.

This divine structure of the city is further emphasized by the alternative names given to the city gates at the ends of the bazaars on which the temples stand. Following Mughal and also earlier Rajput practice, these gates are commonly named after the cities towards which they face; but the Ajmeri Gate is also popularly called Kishan Pol (a local corruption of the name of Krishna, another *avatar* or incarnation of Vishnu), and the Sanganeri Gate is popularly called Shiva Pol.

The two temples described are not alone. They form the base of a ritual triangle, the apex of which is the city's most significant temple, the Govind Deo Mandir, situated at the northern extremity of the palace garden (illus. 39). Even

38 Rama Mandir (with *murtis* of Rama-Sita).

39 View across the palace garden, towards the Govind Deo temple, with the palace axially behind.

today this is by far the most active temple in the city, its importance deriving from the image contained within it (illus. 6). This image, of Krishna as the cowherd Govind, had reputedly been 'found' by a disciple of Chaitanya, the sixteenth-century *guru* who identified the Braj region as the scene of Krishna's youth. The image was originally installed in the great Govind Mandir in Vrindavan, at the heart of the Braj region, specially built for the purpose by Sawai Jai Singh's ancestor Raja Man Singh in 1590 (illus. 26). The image was removed from that temple, anticipating its partial destruction by the iconoclastic Mughal Emperor Aurangzeb in 1669; it was subsequently housed at a succession of secret locations and brought to Amber state in

1714. Finally, it was placed in its present purpose-built temple, which was completed in 1735.[56]

A legend about the temple recounts that the original structure was intended as a palace pavilion, but that the god appeared to Sawai Jai Singh in a vision, demanding residence, and the Maharaja obediently removed himself to the main palace building to the south.[57] This seemingly simple story is significant in various ways. Firstly, it accounts for the building's unusual design: unlike the *shikhara*-topped *nagara* temples described, and equally unlike the more fashionable *haveli*-plan temples, this building is organized like a garden palace pavilion. The external form and the internal disposition of rooms find their closest parallel in palace structures such as the pavilions at Dig, built in the 1760s (a correspondence that later accretions to the temple have disguised but not obliterated). More importantly, the legend underlines the spatial relationship between the temple and the main palace building. The temple stands within a formal garden in front of the palace, axially aligned with its centre, thus establishing a relationship between the god and the palace. The role of the god in the management of the state was made explicit by Sawai Jai Singh, who declared the god to be the real king, while he himself served as his minister or *diwan*.[58] This declaration was not so much a self-dethronement as an elevation of the position of the Maharaja to that of an associate of the god. And this association is visibly marked for all worshippers at the shrine who, on turning from the *murti*, confront the palace. Housing a cult image within the palace area is a common feature of Indian courts: we may recall the presence in the Amber fort of the *murti* (image) of Shila Devi, brought from Bengal by Man Singh I. What is exceptional in the present case is that the image is an object of popular devotion, thus uniting deity, king and people in a single ordered space.

This much is evident from the structures as they stand. A final point to be derived from the legend is more contentious. The location of the temple in the garden to the south of the Tal Katora associates it with the hunting lodge, Jai Niwas, which predates the foundation of the city. The records stating that the image was brought to the state in 1714 also say that it was first placed in a garden close to Amber and soon afterwards moved to another called Jai Niwas,[59] inviting the hypothesis that the hunting lodge, the resting place of the *murti* and the temple are all one and the same. A. K. Roy explicitly ruled out any such identification on grounds of chronology, since the temple was not completed until 1735.[60] But it is feasible that the image was placed in the lodge soon after its

construction in 1713, and that the temple is a conversion, a refashioning of its structure. And the legend could be interpreted as recording these events. If this identification were correct, it would mean that the *murti* was installed on the site before the building of the city began, and this in turn would explain the peculiar importance, insisted on by Sawai Jai Singh, of maintaining Jai Niwas within the city. It would also fulfil the shastric convention of placing a Vishnu temple at the heart of the palace area.[61] It would be a further hypothesis to suggest that this installation of the image on the site before the construction of the city was a premeditated act, intended to counteract the ill effects of the terrain, and to equip it with the kind of sacred associations vital to other Indian city foundations.

Sawai Jai Singh's Observatories

Almost as much as for founding a city, Sawai Jai Singh is remembered today as India's 'astronomer king' and as the builder of the splendid astronomical observatories known as Jantar Mantar (illus. 40, 41). Of these, the largest and best-preserved are in Jaipur (within the palace boundary or *sarahad*) and in Delhi. There is some uncertainty about the dates of their construction. The one in Jaipur appears to have been completed by 1734 but may have been founded as early as 1718,[62] nearly a decade before the founding of the city (and certainly it would have been sensible to construct astronomical instruments on the open plain by the hunting ground rather than in the congested city of Amber). The one in Delhi was built in 1724–5 for the Mughal Emperor, but on land that was owned by Sawai Jai Singh.[63] The third surviving observatory is the miniature one at Benares, constructed by Sawai Jai Singh on the roof of the palace on the Ganges that had been built by his ancestor Raja Man Singh I in the 1590s. In the same period (1724–34) two small observatories were also built at Mathura and Ujjain; the former has all but disappeared and the latter entirely so.[64]

The name 'Jantar Mantar' combines a corruption of *yantra* ('instrument') with a euphonic suffix. The major instruments concerned are the Samrat Yantra, a gigantic sundial in the form of a right-angled triangle with curved wings; and the circular Ram Yantra and the fragmented bowls of the Jai Prakash, both of which are for determining the position of planets. The strong visual appeal of these instruments and (to those not versed in astronomy) their mysterious functions have excited much attention, and Sawai Jai Singh's evidently enthusiastic pursuit of the subject has led to some exaggerations and misunderstandings.

The first point to establish is that the modern Western distinction between astronomy and astrology did not exist in eighteenth-century India: both were parts of the single field known as *jyotish vidya*. The assumption that planetary movements are intimately and causally linked to events in our human lives was central to the prevailing Indian world-view and there is no reason to suppose that Sawai Jai Singh was an exception. It would therefore be quite mistaken to characterize him as a modern empirical scientist, a Galileo struggling against intellectual conservatism and religious superstition. His aim was to improve the accuracy of astronomical observation but his purpose was to apply this knowledge to life, and most especially to the performance of his functions as a king in the domains of religious observance and politics. Understanding the universe was for him a key to understanding the world, not an end in itself.

Sawai Jai Singh's assistant in these matters, indeed his tutor, was a south Indian Brahmin named Jagannath. Together the two men found that the tables of astronomical predictions contained in ancient Indian texts such as *Surya Siddhanta* and *Brahma Siddhanta* contained errors. As these tables determined the Hindu calendar of religious festivals, this mattered very much. They further found that observations could be improved by borrowing some of the techniques of the Arab tradition of astronomy, and, even more significantly, that by designing and building larger and more complex instruments, they could improve even on the Arabic system.

Between them Sawai Jai Singh and Jagannath wrote two major texts. Jagannath's *Samrat Siddhanta*, in Sanskrit, is an attempt to supplement and correct the ancient Indian texts. It is dedicated to his patron, and the political purpose of the study is made immediately plain by the insistence that 'in future, whoever be the Lord of the realm, he should assure himself by making inquiries into the motions of the heavenly bodies by making instruments'.[65] Their other text is the *Zij Muhammad Shahi*, which similarly offers corrections, in this case to the tables found in earlier Islamic works, such as those prepared by the fifteenth-century Timurid 'astronomer king' Ulugh Beg of Samarkand. The preface to this second work was written by Sawai Jai Singh himself and is dedicated to his own imperial overlord, the Mughal Emperor Muhammad Shah. Along with the construction of the Delhi Jantar Mantar, the offering of this text was part of an attempt to persuade the Emperor to revise details of the calendar, 'seeing that very important affairs of state, both regarding religion and the administration of empire, depend upon these'.[66] A preoccupation with astronomy was not therefore merely an individual's passion but an activity deemed appropriate, even essential, for a ruler, and Sawai Jai Singh was exceptional only in the lengths to which he pursued it, designing and building

40 Samrat Yantra, Jantar Mantar, Jaipur.

41 Jai Prakash, Jantar Mantar, Jaipur.

instruments to improve the available measurements.

The extent to which Sawai Jai Singh's interests were guided by European science has been exaggerated. True, he was open to all authority, actively seeking out diverse advanced opinion and practice; and to this end he repeatedly requested and received scientists from the Jesuit mission at Goa. The first, Pedro da Silva Leitao, arrived in 1731 and remained in Jaipur until his death 60 years later, and others had joined him in 1740.[67] But starting as it did after the construction of his first and largest observatories, this embassy cannot have contributed much to his practice. Furthermore, Sawai Jai Singh remained comparatively ill-informed about developments in Europe because the theories of the modern physicists were anathema to his Jesuit informants. He was perfectly aware of ideas from ancient Europe – those of Euclid and Ptolemy – because these had long since entered the Arabic tradition, which was one of his main sources. He had also acquired some modern works, by the French astronomer Philippe La Hire (1640–1718) and the Englishman John Flamsteed (1646–1720), which reflected more recent thinking; but he was not made aware of the force and the European reception of the ideas of Newton, Kepler, Galileo or even Copernicus. So in spite of a likely awareness of the existence of contrary views, he held to the perception of the earth as the fixed centre of the universe.[68]

The other aspect of this subject that is liable to be misunderstood is the relationship between astronomy and town planning in Jaipur. *Vastu vidya* and *jyotish vidya* are two branches of the same tradition of knowledge, and they share much common ground: for example, the directional and planetary associations in the two systems are the same. But this common ground is universal; it is not unique to Jaipur. Nevertheless, some scholars have argued

that Jaipur's ordered plan reflects Sawai Jai Singh's scientific interests,[69] an explanation that again attributes the design to the patron, and that seriously underestimates the organizing capacity of *vastu vidya* itself. More eccentric is the theory proposed by Sten Nilsson that the 15° 'misalignment' of the city's grid has an astronomical explanation: that it brings the city into alignment with the sign of Leo, Sawai Jai Singh's birth sign.[70] Since this theory appears to have gained some ground it is worth addressing. First, the alignment of the city, as already shown, relates to the natural topography of the site, and especially to the ridge across the plain, as anyone who has walked through the city can testify. Second, a divergence from magnetic north by this amount would not be considered a misalignment within the *vastu vidya* system, where north is not a single line but the whole spectrum of the direction lying between north-west and north-east. Thus the elegant coincidence discovered by Nilsson is superfluous. The precise orientation of Jaipur uses the site within the flexible frame of the theoretical base; and the ideal orientation is asserted, as described, through the alignment with Galta's Surya temple. Perhaps even more importantly, Nilsson's theory misrepresents the role of *jyotish* within *vastu vidya*, for quite simply the horoscope of a city does not depend upon the birth sign of its founder but on the time of its foundation, or on the dimensions of its site.[71]

All this is not to suggest that astronomy as practised by Sawai Jai Singh was irrelevant to the city's planning. On the contrary, the two fields of theory are intimately linked in the Indian tradition, and the practice of both was especially highly developed in Jaipur at this time. But their connection there was not a unique phenomenon; it was intrinsic to both systems. Astronomy is therefore not the special 'theme' or 'concept' of Jaipur. It is a branch of

42 The palace at Amber.

thought that was related to architecture here as everywhere in pre-colonial India.

The Palace

This study now moves from the macro level of town planning to the micro level of individual buildings, with a focus on those that compose the palace. Aside from the constraints presented by the site itself, the town plan has been explained in the two related contexts of the theoretical paradigm and historical precedents, the latter being somewhat less prominent because of the comparative paucity of historical opportunites for planning and building

whole cities on fresh sites. In the case of the palace, the precedents are far more numerous and the Jaipur City Palace owes much of its design to a long-running Rajput palace tradition, of which surviving examples date from the mid-fifteenth century (the palace in Chitor of Rana Kumbha) to the previous palace of the state rulers in Amber (illus. 42).[72] At the same time, however, the Jaipur palace reaches beyond these antecedents to realize elements of the theoretical paradigm that were not always so successfully achieved.

The indigenous conception of a palace involves a sequence of enclosures of increasing impenetrability from the public outer sphere to the inner

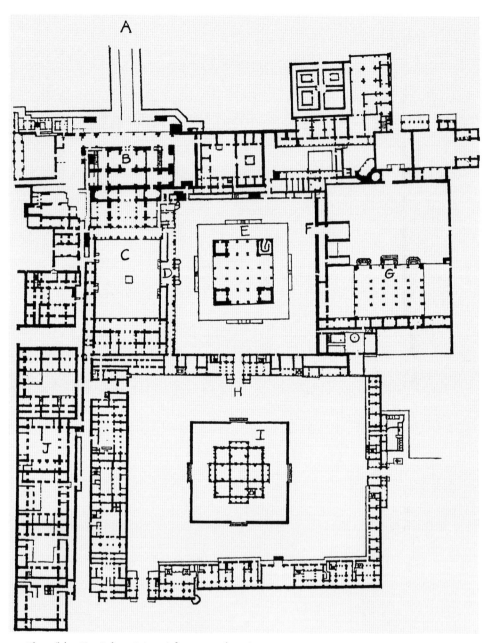

43 Plan of the City Palace, Jaipur (after B. L. Dhama).

A Garden
B Chandra Mahal
C Pritam Nivas Chowk
D Ganesh Pol
E Sarvato Bhadra
F Amba Pol
G Sabha Nivas
H Rajendra Pol
I Mubarak Mahal
J Zenana.

44 The Chandra Mahal of the City Palace, photographed by Raja Deen Dayal in 1876.

apartments of the king and of his women.[73] Sometimes these enclosures are visualized as concentric zones, each marked by its own boundary wall (illus. 18). For example, a large eighteenth-century painting depicting the Court of Vishnu, now housed in the Chandra Mahal,[74] shows an arrangement reminiscent of the plan of the temple at Srirangam, with seven walls, each with a *gopura* or gate-tower in the centre of each side, thus creating four sequences of seven gates. Alternatively, the courtyards may be arranged in a linear series, as in the Jaipur palace (illus. 43). The sense of progressing towards a protected centre is maintained, and the visitor approaching from the main, eastern entrance, still passes through a sequence of seven gates.

The first of these gates is the Sireh Deorhi or 'boundary door', located at the centre of the eastern side of the palace *sarahad*, on the public bazaar which takes its name. It is painted pink, like all of the other main structures along the street. Aligned with it but some distance within is the Naqqarwal ka Darwaza (illus. 13). The name indicates its function as the drum house, and it is equipped with a musicians' gallery, from where the players announced the arrivals and departures of the Maharaja. Like most of the original palace buildings, this is painted not pink but a creamy yellow. It gives access to the large open square of the Jaleb Chowk, bordered by a variety of palace offices. Directly aligned again, but on the opposite side of Jaleb Chowk, is the third gate,

45 18th-century apartments around the Moti Mahal Chowk
in the fort of Mehrangarh, in Jodhpur.

Udai Pol, still facing east and named after the
rising sun.

Immediately within the Udai Pol are two more
gates, close together. The similarly named Vijay
Pol and Jay Pol are architecturally less impressive.
The axial scheme is temporarily abandoned here,
and these gates are constricting passages designed
to impede an invading force. They turn us
southward and deliver us into a small courtyard in
front of the later Diwan-i-Am (or Sabha Nivas;
illus 43 G). From here the path continues westward,
as the next gate, the Amba Pol, is a doorway
leading off the western side of this court and into
the large courtyard of the building now known as

the Sarvato Bhadra. Facing this again on the
western side is the last gate in the sequence, the
splendid Ganesh Pol, named after the guardian
deity of households; this leads into the private
courtyard in front of the Chandra Mahal, the main
palace structure (illus. 14 and 15).[75]

The conventional and auspicious seven-fold
scheme, thus satisfactorily resolved horizontally,
was applied vertically too. The shastric texts specify
seven storeys for the palaces of Kshatriya kings,[76]
and the Chandra Mahal is one of the few Rajput
palaces to achieve this paradigmatic number (illus.
44). On the ground floor is the Pritam Nivas, with a
small audience hall in its centre. The next two

46 The Jas Mandir and garden in the palace at Amber.

storeys are occupied by the magnificent Sukh Nivas, of double height internally but expressed as two storeys on the outer façades. Above this is the Rang Mahal, also known as the Shobha Nivas, with coloured glasswork; then the Chhavi Nivas with its blue-painted interiors, the Shri Nivas with the *sheesh mahal* (palace of mirrors) and finally the crowning pavilion of the Mukut Mandir.[77] Multi-storeyed palaces certainly feature in earlier Rajput palace design – those at Udaipur and Bundi (both built over long time-spans) are amongst the many precedents – but the various storeys are rarely so clearly delineated as here, nor so faithful to the number seven. The Govind Mandir at Datia (1625)

has a five-storeyed tower standing over a two-storeyed substructure; but only the lesser-known Juna Mahal at Dungarpur, built in the sixteenth century, is so clearly articulated as a seven-storeyed structure.

The individual forms and motifs that make up the language of this architecture – the types of column, arch, balcony and opening – all belong to the continuing Rajput palace tradition, and are directly comparable to similar components of contemporary buildings in Jodhpur, Bikaner, Jaisalmer, Udaipur and elsewhere throughout the Rajput region (illus. 45). There is here no characteristic Jaipur 'order' or style of arch. At this

47 The Mughal-style garden to the north of the Chandra Mahal.

micro level the architectural vocabulary is simply the regional style of the time.

The overall symmetry and unity of massing of the Chandra Mahal, on the other hand, is a less standard feature. More often Rajput designers allowed for, indeed seemed to relish, asymmetry and irregularity. The great palaces in the cities just named, for example, have no such coherence in their outlines. But the greater compactness of the Chandra Mahal is not without precedent. The courtyard palaces of Orchha and Datia, built in the sixteenth and early seventeenth centuries, are well-known precedents that achieve symmetry in their form and external massing. And these are not as exceptional as is often supposed: they belong to an alternative tradition of Rajput palace design that stretches back to the palace of Ratan Singh in Chitor (*c.* 1530) and to the Man Mandir in Gwalior (*c.* 1500). So the Chandra Mahal draws on and extends design ideas that were long established within the Rajput school.

The palace also makes specific references to the immediate and local precedent at Amber, the palace that was necessarily abandoned by Sawai Jai Singh and which in some respects is recreated here. There are several indications of such an intention. The use of creamy yellow paint, to distinguish the palace from the surrounding buildings of the city, establishes a connection with the similarly coloured walls of Amber. The crowning Mukut Mandir has a *bangaldar* roof between two round domes, replicating the roof of the seventeenth-century Jas

48 The Sarvato Bhadra (originally the hall of public audience).

Mandir at Amber (illus. 46). On the ground floor, a pool of water spills out into a formal garden (to the north of the palace) as in the Sukh Nivas at Amber, though in this instance there is an even more explicit debt to Mughal models since the garden is a *charbagh* (a four-part garden divided by water channels) and thus follows a type that was imported from Persia by the Mughals in the sixteenth century (illus. 47).

The garden sounds a note of Mughal influence that becomes more pronounced with some of the later additions to the palace, and especially the audience hall in the court to the east (illus. 48). This hall was added almost immediately, within the reign of Sawai Jai Singh.[78] Departing from the model of the multi-storeyed tower, it is an independent pavilion, comparable to those of Shah Jahan's palace in the seventeenth-century fort in Delhi (illus. 49). Its architectural style and the use of pink rather than cream paint enhance the similarity, and again suggest an intention to create a court to rival and even displace that of the Mughal overlord. Such imitation of Mughal buildings does not necessarily signal an abandonment of the original and indigenous conceptions: the very fact of an extension towards the east is consistent with shastric norms.[79]

This hall is now known locally as the Diwan-i-Khas or, to use the indigenous vocabulary, Sarvato Bhadra, implying its use as a private audience hall. It is clear, however, that private audiences were originally held in the ground floor of the Chandra Mahal, in the heart of the palace, as the French

49 The Diwan-i-Am in the Red Fort of Delhi; built in the 1640s.

traveller Louis Rousselet recorded.[80] This outer hall was therefore conceived as a grand ceremonial Hall of Public Audience (a Diwan-i-Am, or Sabha Nivas), which accounts for both its architectural pretentions and the spacious courtyard around it. Only the subsequent construction of an additional, yet larger hall, to the east again and closer to the entrance to the palace,[81] caused the 'demotion' of the first to 'private' status. A passage from the *Pratap Prakash* of Krishnadatta Kavi presents a colourful picture of this hall in use at the end of the eighteenth century:

> Orders are then issued for arrangements of the general (public) durbar. The *darogha* (director) conveys information to all *deorhis* (gates of the palace). Hundreds of *naqibs* (runners) run off to intimate the rajas of different places, nobles and others belonging to the king's clan. The *Sabhanivas* (durbar hall) is furnished with seven coloured durries, and sheets, as white as moonlight, are spread over them. *Mirfarshas* (weights) studded with gems are put to press the corners of the floor-spreads. The silver canopy supported by diamond-encrusted pillars and decorated with emerald pendants is spread and tied fast with silken strings. A velvet *gaddi* (king's seat) is arranged under it with *ʒarwaf* (gold embroidered) pillows. Curtains are hung on all sides of the *Sabhanivas* and *saibans*

50 The Jal Mahal.

(cloth-sheds) are spread outside to cover the open courtyard. The nobles and courtiers take their seats in rows assigned to them . . . The king is apprised of their presence. He puts on the durbar costumes: turban, *chhonga*, *turra* and *kalangi* (plumes of pearls), *kiran rumal* (scarf), an embroidered *jama*, earrings with white, red and bluish pearls representing *Shukra* (Venus), *Mangala* (Mars) and *Budha* (Mercury), an embroidered and embedded *partala* (belt), *aliband* to stick the shield to his waist, a dagger tied up, and he holds a long sword called *dhoop* in his hand. Thus the Lord of Amber proceeds to the durbar hall followed and attended by hundreds of his bodyguards, *khawasas* and officials. The water-man carries *Gangajala* (Ganges water) in a *jhari* (a decorative water container), an attendant holds the golden *qalamdan* (ink-stand), while others bearing swords, shields, *gurza* (mace), *sotas pankhis* and *adanis* (the royal fans) follow him. When the Maharaja enters the durbar hall the *chobdar* (herald) announces his arrival; the nobles and courtiers salute him, the pandits and poets offer their benedictions. Then he adorns the royal *gaddi* and attends to state business and petitions submitted by the representatives of different states. He then turns to the *gunijanas* (artistes). The pandits have their discussions of the six schools of philosophy, the poets recite their eulogical poems, the bards read aloud the glory of the family, and the musicians perform the six *ragas* and thirty *raginis*. After holding durbar for one *pahar* (three hours) the king retires via the *Sarvatobhadra* and all the courtiers are granted permission to leave.[82]

FURTHER ADDITIONS

Three further palace structures from the eighteenth century now need to be considered. The first is the outlying Jal Mahal or water palace, built in the centre of the artificial lake outside the city to the north-east, by the road to Amber (illus. 50). Though sometimes dated as late as 1775,[83] it is likely that this was constructed by Sawai Jai Singh, at the time of foundation, around 1734. Certainly, one surviving drawing in the palace collection that shows it is of a type and style consistent with other drawings from Sawai Jai Singh's time.[84] The Jal Mahal is a pleasure resort. Its position in a lake extends an established Rajput tradition, of which earlier examples include the very early Palace of Padmini at Chitor (originally built *c.* 1300 but reconstructed *c.* 1880) and the Jag Mandir at Udaipur (1620s). Roughly contemporary is the Jag Nivas, also at Udaipur, which was built by Maharana Jagat Singh II (*r.* 1734–51).

Two conspicuous additions to the main palace buildings within the city were made by Sawai Jai Singh's successors later in the eighteenth century. The founder died in September 1743. His immediate successor was his eldest son, Ishvari Singh (*r.* 1743–50). Throughout his reign, however, Ishvari Singh was plagued by the counter-claim of his younger half-brother Madho Singh. Invoking the unstated but mutually agreed terms of the treaty with Udaipur that had restored Kachchwaha authority in 1708, Madho Singh claimed that as the son of a Sisodia princess he was the rightful heir. The agreement made tacitly by Sawai Jai Singh had come to haunt his son. Madho Singh secured military assistance from Udaipur, Bundi and the Holkar Marathas, to enforce his claim, but his attempts to gain the throne by force in 1744 and 1748 failed, and in 1749 Ishvari Singh constructed a victory tower, the Ishvar Lat, to proclaim his defeat of the pretender and his allies. This tall, graceful tower stands on the southern perimeter of the *sarahad*, in a central and dominant position in the city.

But the persistent Madho Singh did not relinquish his efforts. Indeed wider Rajput polity was dominated throughout the 1730s and '40s by this succession dispute and a related struggle over Bundi. In 1729 Sawai Jai Singh had intervened in the affairs of Bundi and dethroned the ruler, Buddh Singh, in favour of a pliable young relative. In an attempt to recover his kingdom in 1734, the dispossessed Raja sought the aid of Holkar and Scindia, thus initiating Maratha involvement in Rajput territories. The campaign was not successful but it encouraged Sawai Jai Singh to make his own diplomatic overtures to the Maratha Peshwa, Baji Rao. When Buddh Singh died in 1739, the cause was taken up by his son Umed Singh, who regained his patrimony by degrees between 1744 and 1748. Umed Singh was naturally willing to form an alliance with Madho Singh, who claimed to be similarly dispossessed, and against Sawai Jai Singh's elder son.

The motives of the ruler of Udaipur, Maharana Jagat Singh II, are harder to fathom, but plainly they went beyond a desire to enforce the terms of the original treaty. The whole struggle has been interpreted by the Jaipur specialist G. N. Bahura as a measure of the Udaipur Maharana's jealousy of Jaipur's power and his desire to weaken it, using

Madho's claim as a pretext.[85] Equally, it might be seen as an indication of the Maharana's desire not to lessen but to harness that power for his own ends, using his relative as the agent. The great prize was Jaipur's economic strength, which continued to grow, and was augmented at this time through the establishment of a flourishing paper-making industry at Sanganer. The wealth of Jaipur would have been of considerable use to Udaipur in meeting the demands of the tribute exacted by the Marathas, and to this end a client–king would have served well. The sustained conflict evidently demoralized Ishvari Singh and he committed suicide in 1750, leaving the way clear for Madho Singh, who ruled from 1751 to 1768. The destruction of the tower that had been built to humiliate him would have been too obvious an action, and instead Madho Singh fabricated the improbable myth (still current in Jaipur) that the tower had originally been built to enable Ishvari Singh to spy on a local beauty at her ablutions.

Madho Singh was succeeded by his infant son Prithvi Singh, who ruled for a decade (1768–78) before being succeeded by his own brother Pratap Singh (r. 1778–1803). Pratap was a man rather more in the image of the founder, his grandfather Sawai Jai Singh. Though not on the same scale, he was an enthusiastic patron of literature, painting and architecture. His major addition to the palace is the building for which Jaipur is best known today, the Hawa Mahal, constructed at the south-eastern corner of the *sarahad* in 1799.[86] The designer of this remarkable structure has been identified as one Lal Chand Ustad.[87] Though often described as merely a screen, the Hawa Mahal is in fact a structure built around two courtyards, but with a vast screen-like façade on the east, overlooking the street (illus. 16 and 51). Intended as a place from where women of the court could view ceremonial events in this most public of thoroughfares, this is the element on which the builders lavished most attention. Admired by many for its breathtaking eccentricity, the Hawa Mahal has been derided by others as a gratuitous flourish, disconnected from any serious purpose. Leaving aside arguments as to its quality,[88] what we wish to stress here is that the seeming confusion and jumble of forms is in fact regulated by a strict and carefully calculated order. Though superficially it appears arbitrary, a careful scrutiny will reveal how even here the architect has devised a composition out of a handful of well-established and elementary principles. As an example of *vastu vidya* in practice, it is worth analysing in some detail.

Running down the central vertical spine of the façade is the repeated motif of a triple-bayed opening. This motif is a simplification of a standard pavilion type, which is often found as a crowning element – as in the Mukut Mandir on top of the Chandra Mahal – comprising two square, domed *chhatris* (small pavilions) flanking a rectangular *chhatri* with a curved *bangaldar* roof. These components are here reduced and fused to make a triple window. On either side of this motif is a smaller one, again a triple opening, but here expressed as three sides of an octagonal turret, capped by a round dome. Divisions into three are common in Indian design, usually with the central part wider than the outer two. Here the two motifs are each divisible into three, with (in the case of the first one) a wider central part.

The grouping of the motifs follows the same principle. If we label the first motif 'A' and the second 'b', then the framing of 'A' by two 'b's creates the larger three-element unit 'bAb', of which the central element is the widest. Furthermore, the rhythm of the motifs' repetition across the entire façade can be expressed as the

51 The Hawa Mahal.

sequence: 'bAbbAbAbAbbAb'. Why this pattern? Taking a group of three ('bAb') as a unit, the horizontal rhythm resolves itself again into three parts: 'bAb–bAbAbAb–bAb'. The central part is wider, containing three of the 'A' motifs rather than just one (just as, in pavilions such as the Mukut Mandir, the central *chhatri* is itself subdivided to give three openings rather than one). At the critical points to the left and right, the 'b' motif is repeated to give emphasis and to distinguish the central from the flanking groups.

This pattern of repetition, based on elaborations of tripling, is then repeated vertically three times to create three identical storeys. What then of the remaining two storeys, and why five in total? The composition requires a top. The number has to be kept odd, and fewer than the seven of the Chandra Mahal so as not to rival its height. The top two storeys here provide a crown to the main three. The fourth storey repeats the pattern again, but with slight variations in height between the elements, to allow for the curved skyline of the fifth, which echoes on the largest scale the outline of the *bangaldar* roof that is contained in the originating central motif.

The whole composition, in short, is worked out on a carefully regulated grid, applying compositional principles that were previously well established both textually and in practice. These principles are tripartite division, subdivision of the wider centre, framing, grouping, repetition and the relation of the whole to the part. It is important to recognize that applying these principles will not always produce an identical result. Depending on how they are applied, they can be used to achieve any one of an indefinite number of possible compositions. The Hawa Mahal is merely one possible outcome, derived from – not determined by – the principles. It is our contention that the compositions of all traditional Indian buildings[89] can be explained in terms of these and similar principles; in this sense *vastu vidya* can be described as a universal system.

52 Detail of the courtyard, Ramachandra Temple (illus. 60).

3 The Courts of Ramachandra

The previous chapter looked at Jaipur from the city's foundation in 1727 to the end of the eighteenth century. We moved in scale between a macro level – describing the city plan as a whole – and a micro level, analysing individual buildings, including the Hawa Mahal. In the present chapter, the purpose is similar, but the range of the scale shifts downwards: at the macro level we consider a single building complex, and at the micro level we examine some of its smallest component parts and motifs, to demonstrate how *vastu vidya* informs all levels of design. Historically, we move ahead to the mid-nineteenth century. The building selected is the Ramachandra Temple, situated on the eastern side of Sireh Deori Bazaar, opposite the entrance to the palace (illus. 119). The temple was built under the patronage of Maiji Sahiba Sri Chandrawatji, the mother of Maharaja Sawai Ram Singh II (r. 1835–80), in 1854, the year in which the young Maharaja, who had succeeded to the throne as a minor, was invested with ruling powers. It is possible that the construction of the temple under royal patronage was intended to mark the waning of the Rajmata's political power and an appropriate turning of her attention to religious affairs. It is a courtyard temple with a shrine originally containing a *murti* (image) of Ramachandra. Until recently the *garbha griha* (literally 'womb-house', the shrine housing the *murti*) still contained a picture of Rama-Sita, but its central position has been surrendered to

murtis of Krishna-Radha. Since 1865 the complex has also housed a Sanskrit college. We have chosen this building as an example to explore in detail partly because of the high resolution and rich design of this multi-functional complex, and partly because of the historical moment it represents, just before the introduction into Jaipur's building practice of the influence of European architectural ideas – a story that is taken up in Chapter Four.

Today there are various ways of understanding and describing the design of the Ramachandra Temple. Insofar as it belongs to the pre-Modern era, it can obviously be described as 'traditional', but depending on the preferences of the interested observer, the understanding of 'traditional' principles veers between a rationale of climate response and social need, and one that regards composition in terms of volumes and light. One of the main objectives of this exercise for the designer of today is to extract a few identifying essentials:

> Abstracting elements from the past in order to derive building form from it constitutes what we call 'abstract regionalism'. It is a very difficult and fine line to follow. It mainly incorporates the abstract qualities of a building, for example, massing, solids and void, proportions, sense of space, use of light, and structural principles in their reinterpreted form. It also endeavours to bring back to existence

the cultural issues. An attempt is made to define in terms of design elements the prevalent culture of the region concerned.[1]

This dualistic view encompasses aesthetic and sociological elements, which in the quotation above are labelled 'abstract qualities' and 'cultural issues', but are sometimes called the 'spiritual' and the 'physical' aspects of traditional design. B. V. Doshi explains his own response to pre-industrial architecture, including that of Jaipur:

> At the physical level, it embodied centuries of learning with regard to orientation, climate, building materials and construction techniques. At the spiritual level, the built form conveyed total harmony with the life-style in all its daily as well as seasonal rituals, unifying the socio-cultural and religious aspirations of the individual and the community. To achieve this unity and to integrate physical and spiritual needs, due importance was given to nature and its basic laws. Nature was accepted as it is . . . The compactness of the town plan, building using thick walls with niches, and a variety of in-between elements like balconies, incorporated both the symbolic as well as social meaning. Jaisalmer, old Jaipur and old Delhi are testimonies to such thinking.[2]

While it is certainly true of the buildings of Jaipur that their architectural forms convey meaning, both symbolic and social, the same could be said of all architecture, at all times, at all places. What such explanations of the peculiarities of traditional Indian design fail to acknowledge is the role of a highly developed discipline, or theory of design. While it may be intellectually stimulating to deconstruct traditional design in terms of solids and voids and spiritual qualities, it does not lead to an understanding of the tools and methods that formed the basis of its architectural expression. The main purpose of this chapter is to demonstrate that traditional buildings such as the Ramachandra Temple can be explained, and their appreciation enriched, by the use of the theoretical basis that informed their design. Every aspect of its architectural vocabulary, from the overall plan to the smallest detail, can be understood in terms of its own language.

The General Plan

The Ramachandra Temple is a multifunctional temple complex that also houses a Sanskrit college. The site rises steeply towards the east, and measures 93 *hasta* x 113 *hasta* (1 *hasta* = *c*. 45 cm), with the shorter side (or width) abutting the Sireh Deori Bazaar.[3] The temple complex faces west, towards the palace, for it would be inappropriate for the deity to have its back to the palace. In accordance with one of the planning principles of the streets of Jaipur in general, shops of a uniform size on the ground floor present a uniform façade at the street level. The shop modules are made of two square bays of 5 *hasta*, which means that each shop measures 5 x 10 *hasta*. Thus, the initiating factors of the design process include the functional programme of a religious-cum-educational institute, the rectangular, sloping site, and the side being adjacent to a main road lined with shops that form its front (illus. 53).

Obviously, the entrance to the complex is from the road. The shorter side faces the road, an arrangement found throughout Jaipur, to allow the maximum number of plots to gain direct access. This side, which is strictly speaking the width of the plot, is accordingly considered the front of the site and provides the basic dimension. To calculate the precise point of entry, this side is subdivided into nine parts, and depending on the direction it faces, the corresponding peripheral deities mark the suitable and unsuitable entry points.[4] For a west-facing house, the central division of the nine is marked by Varuna, and is the suitable part for the main door. This procedure treats the width of the site as one side of the *vastu purusha mandala*, and derives the meanings of the other subdivisions from the corresponding presiding deities. For a temple, the door should be in alignment with its *garbha griha* door, and so is always in the centre,[5] irrespective of the direction the temple faces; but as it happens in this case, the centre would be appropriate anyhow.

The defining side of any plot is its width also because the length is its derivative. The width may be rationalized in terms of a set of normative dimensions, and then used as the key dimension of the plot. For example, the ideal widths for the house of a king are 108, 100, 92, 84 or 76 *hasta*, and the corresponding preferred lengths are 135, 125, 115, 104 and 95 *hasta*. Here the length is one and a quarter times the width.[6] The established width is treated as one side of the *mandala*, and the length of the plot as its other side. It does not matter that the *mandala* is a square while the plot is actually rectangular, because it is the equality of the subdivisions of each side that matters. The dimensions of the idealized square *mandala* take on tangible form in the dimensions of the plot. It is not only the length that is derived from the width, but the height of the house,[7] the height of the door[8] and the width of the courtyard.[9] In fact, every co-ordinate that subdivides the site into spatial units is generated first and foremost by subdividing the width. So, arriving at a suitable, workable and dividable width is crucial. The network of lines that is generated by the division of the plot corresponds to the lines of the idealized organization grid of the *mandala*. Since the primary role of the *vastu purusha mandala* is as a mental design tool, it does not matter how closely it matches the *mandala* in its geometry.

The largest span that the building complex of the Ramachandra Temple affords is 10 *hasta*. The recommended width of a room or a range is 17 *hasta* for large mansions, 10 *hasta* for medium sized buildings and 5 *hasta* for small buildings.[10] These

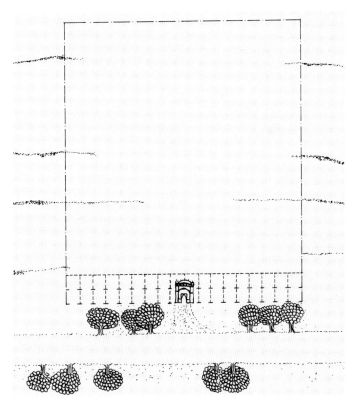

53 Reconstruction of the site for the Ramchandra temple.

suitable widths may be related to the available stone lengths used for spanning the roof, but are clearly not exclusively dependent on one slab size. The roof may use materials other than stone slabs, such as the six types of roof covering popular in the time of Mandan: thatch, leaves, slabs of timber or stone, bamboo, wattle, mud and stone blocks (or perhaps bricks).[11] Stone slabs are recommended for the king's house only.[12] Another method of calculating the width of a *shala* (range) is by adding 70 to the width of the plot and dividing the result by 14.[13] So, if a plot measures 100 *hasta* in width, then the width of its constituent *shala* is about 12 *hasta*. In fact, any of the suggested widths will result in a room size between 17 and 5 *hasta*, and most are around the mean of 10 *hasta*. In establishing the width, not only the building materials but also design ideas – such as the *vastu purusha mandala* – need to be taken into account. That is to say, the width, when divided into 9 (to rationalize the plot in terms of the recommended *mandala* of 81 squares), must yield a viable subdivision within the recommended range. In fact the width of the plot may influence the kind of design grid one uses to subdivide it. So the question is clear: how many divisions can the width support in order to be both structurally feasible, and, more importantly, conceptually desirable?

The given width of 93 *hasta* can easily accommodate nine divisions of 10 *hasta* each; whereas a higher division of ten parts would require a larger width of 100 *hasta*, and a lower division of eight would leave too large a gap of 13 *hasta*. Also, it is easier to work with an odd-numbered division, as the entrance gateway is to be centrally placed. So the most appropriate division in this case is of nine parts. The shop-lined front therefore accommodates two shops per bay, with eight shop fronts on either side of the entrance gateway, which uses two shop widths.

All of the nine divisions are potential co-ordinates that could flow along the length of the building and map out the skeletal walls of the structure. Thus, the central three divisions accommodate the string of main courtyards, and the next divisions, on either side, accommodate the ranges that surround those courtyards. Together, this makes the central spine of the complex, which occupies five divisions in all. The remaining two divisions on either side house ancillary courtyards, which share the ranges of the central courtyards (illus. 54).

The basic arrangement that emerges is this series of courtyards, with ranges around them. But what are the defining principles that control their arrangement? How are the nine co-ordinates that flow from the width contained to form a mesh of built and open spaces? The answers are to be found in the way the ranges and courtyards are classified and combined in theory. A *shala* is a continuous range or a room under a single roof form. On an ideal square plot an *ek-shala* (or a house containing a single range or room under one roof) may occupy any side of the square, stretched along its entire length. Wise men must not construct a *shala* without an *alind* or veranda and a *dvar* or door.[14] The way in which the *shala* combines with the *alind* and the *dvar* yields its various types (*prastara*).[15] The remaining area of the plot is the *angan* or *chowk* (courtyard). When this area too is covered, it is called the *garbha griha*.[16] *Dvishala*, as the name suggests, is a house of two ranges, which may be positioned on any adjacent two of the four sides, or any two opposite sides of the square or plot. However, the type with *shalas* on the southern and western sides is preferred,[17] with the *karn*[18] or corner room in the south-west corner. The arrangement where only one side of the square plot is without a *shala* is called *tri-shala*. As the name suggests, it comprises three ranges; the types without an eastern or northern range are preferred.[19] The *chatuh-shala* has four ranges covering all four sides.

Further combinations of these four basic types yield models with five, six, seven, eight, nine or ten ranges, and their combination with verandas, doors, windows, internal rooms and galleries generates further types. The texts classify *shalas* with a maximum of ten ranges: a *dash-shala*. A classic arrangement of a *dash-shala* house is structured around three courtyards in tandem with each other, with ranges on all four sides, and where two opposing ranges of the central courtyard open onto two courtyards each. But, a ten-range model may comprise sets of 4+2+4 ranges, or 3+3+3+1 ranges, or 3+4+3 ranges (illus. 55).[20] So, how does one arrangement differ from another, as all three types have three courtyards with surrounding ranges, creating a mass of building with voids? And how is a courtyard different from any other open space within a building?

In the classic arrangement of a ten-*shala* house, two of the ranges look onto two courtyards each: but they may or may not respond to the visual

54 The linear division of the site.

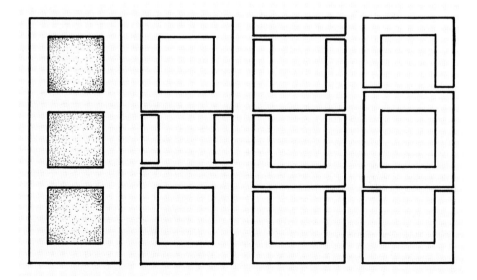

55 Alternative configurations of ranges to define courtyards.

vocabulary of the other three ranges in those courtyards. They may even visually choose to defy their structural commitment to their constituent sets. One of the key features of a courtyard is that the surrounding ranges open into it through the transitional space of an *alind* or veranda. This perforated space may be incorporated within the *shala* as a *shatdaru*, a gallery of columns facing the courtyard. The 'squareness' of the courtyard is established literally by its shape but also metaphorically by the visual correspondence between the four façades. And then there are elements that tie the surrounding walls together: by encircling the courtyard, binding the four sides together with a continuous line, as the plinth and the *chhajja* do; and by mirroring the proportion and shapes of motifs on opposing walls, as the openings do. So the constituent sets of a *dash-shala* emerge from the way their architectural vocabulary is articulated around the three courtyards. One method is to follow the idea of mirroring or echoing the facing elements.

It is this idea of corresponding arrangements that is embodied in the concept of *vedh* (literally 'obstacle'). For example, the *Vishvakarma Prakash* suggests that a house without openings is blind; that one with openings in the wrong directions is partially sighted; one without proper limbs is hunchbacked; one with its door under ground is deaf; and one with openings placed arbitrarily is without direction. Apart from indicating that doors and windows are like the ears and eyes of the house, this also emphasizes the alignment of elements.[21] *Samarangana Sutradhara* maintains that columns, doors and walls must not be opposites, so columns must face columns and doors face doors, and neither must face a blank wall.[22]

The courtyard is the central area, and whether covered or open, it is ruled by the deity Brahma,

and so it is the *brahmasthana*, the place of Brahma. According to *Vishvakarma Prakash*, if there is a column in the centre of the house, it is called a *brahma-vedh*: a violation of Brahma. A wall must never be constructed in the central part of the house, because it violates the *brahmasthana*. The householder must make every effort to protect this area.[23] The central area of a *vastu purusha mandala* where the diagonals intersect is the most vulnerable point, and 'hurting' this must be avoided.[24] In a 64-square *mandala*, the area of the central four plots around the intersection of the diagonals must be protected, and in an 81-square *mandala* the *brahmasthana* covers the central nine squares.[25] The protection of the *brahmasthana* ensures the protection of the central courtyard from any encroachment.

Another crucial aspect of the massing is the proportional relation between the central open space and the covered building. Obviously, the size of the *brahmasthana* changes with the size of the *mandala*. Second, as a rule of thumb, the open area of a courtyard is equivalent to that of the covered *shalas* around it. The width of the courtyard is half the width of the site.[26] The *vidhi* or method of design of a *griha* or house is also followed for the design of a *prasada* or temple.[27] A *prasada*, however, also requires a *garbha griha*, a *pradakshina patha* (circumambulating path) around it, a door measuring a fifth of its width, a *mukha mandapa* (hall) in front and equal to the *garbha griha*, and *shikharas* that are twice the height of the walls of the *garbha griha*.[28]

Returning to the central string of courtyards in the Ramachandra Temple, the first one that the visitor encounters on entry to the complex is at a lower level than the other two. This difference of level, apart from exploiting the slope of the site, provides a separate and a more public courtyard for the college and the offices. The temple might have been placed in front, to gain from the public access to the road, and the college at the back, away from the noise and bustle of the street. But this would have been a violation: the college has to be in the front and on the sides, and the temple at the back with the deity at the farthest point of the site, so that the entire building is under its auspicious gaze. Secondly, placing the temple in the front would make its position on a lower level. The temple has to be situated at the highest level of the site, with nothing built on top or below its *garbha griha*. Therefore, the functional requirements and the features of the site demand a string of at least three courtyards: one at a lower level, another at a higher level, and the third that forms the *garbha griha*.

The grand steps in the first courtyard lead towards the temple – to the second courtyard, through a range that encloses the first courtyard, but which addresses the second in terms of its openings and the articulation of its divisions. This second courtyard belongs to the temple, serving as an open-air *nat mandir*, a space for music and dance performances, and to accommodate large congregations during festivals. This four-range courtyard has opposing façades in dialogue with each other – echoing and mirroring divisions and punctuation, within consistent vertical and horizontal bands predicated by the division of the width of the site. The eastern range of this courtyard has three lofty double-height arches that lead to the third and final courtyard. This is a *garbha griha*, a covered courtyard, with a room for the deity, a *pradakshina patha* around it, and an equally sized *mukha mandapa* in front of it – all the basic elements of a temple.

In the three-courtyard arrangement of the Ramachandra Temple the first common range supports the entrance to the temple on its outer side, but is visually committed to the second courtyard; and the second common range responds to two courtyards – to the second, and to the third; and this ultimate courtyard, which is covered and is the *garbha griha* of the temple, has not a range, but a *pradakshina patha* encasing its eastern side. There cannot be a *shala* behind the *garbha griha*, as anyone using it would be in the unfortunate position of being on the wrong side of the deity. Therefore, the overall arrangement is of a *nav-shala* or nine-range *griha mandir*: 3+4+2 (illus. 56).

The final question to be answered about the plan is why only five of the available nine divisions are used for the central courtyards. In order to avoid *vedh* (violation) between doors and columns, one must not place doors above columns, columns above doors or two doors above one door; and one must not employ an even number of divisions and an odd number of columns in a row.[29] An odd number of divisions also makes it possible to place the entrance centrally, a critical requirement for a temple. So, the choice is between using all of the nine divisions, seven, five, three or one. It is also clearly established that the temple complex would require at least three courtyards in a row, out of which the two forming the *garbha griha* (with the *mukha mandapa*) and the *nat-mandir* have to be exactly aligned.[30] In order to use the typology of courtyards with surrounding ranges, a minimum of three divisions is required. But this minimum would yield narrow tubes of open space, and so would not make optimum use of the available space. Seven divisions would leave the side ranges either without an open space, or with the centrality of their courtyards lost. And in any case, using either seven or all of the nine divisions of the width would spoil the dimensions of the internal courtyards, since they would have a depth shorter than their width. Using the central five divisions, by contrast, not only makes the best possible use of the space but

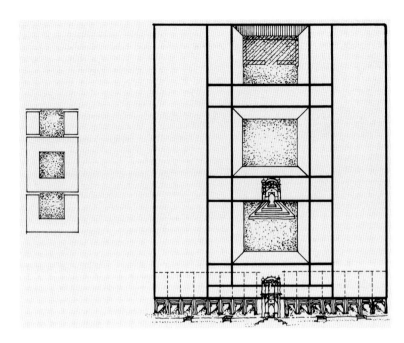

56 Schematic depiction of the Ramachandra temple as a nine-range complex.

also leaves the side ranges with an adequate area for an arrangement of separate courtyards, as well as ensuring the proportional integrity of the main courtyards and ranges (illus. 57 and 58).

The Central Courtyard

The central courtyard is surrounded by two pairs of opposite façades that echo each other in design, creating a dialogue between the facing walls (illus. 59, 60, 62, 63, 120). The concept of *vedh* (violation) and *takabandi* (visual harmony) is carefully pursued by ensuring that each element of the façade is visually 'answered' by a similar or complementary feature directly opposite, and by maintaining the primary axes in the division of the façades. Each side of the courtyard is subdivided into an odd number of elements. The western and the eastern sides are divided into three main divisions, flanked on either side by two smaller portions; the northern

and the southern sides are subdivided into five main divisions, flanked on either side by the same two smaller portions, thus also achieving a resolution of the corners between the two planes (illus. 64). An odd-numbered subdivision places the emphasis on the central element. Each subdivision is also designed along its own central axis. The central division, as a rule, is larger than the adjacent divisions, even if only by an *angula* (*c.* 2 cm). On the lower floor of the western façade, all three main subdivisions have the same pattern – a *bangaldar* roof with domed *chhatris* on either side in relief – but the central opening, which is the main entrance to the courtyard, is significantly larger than the other two. The raised *munavat* (relief) work below the curve of the *bangaldar* of the main opening is more intricate in decoration (as compared to the recessed decoration of the other two) with peacocks, flowers and vases; the horizontal bands follow a rhythm to create a central box – a perfect

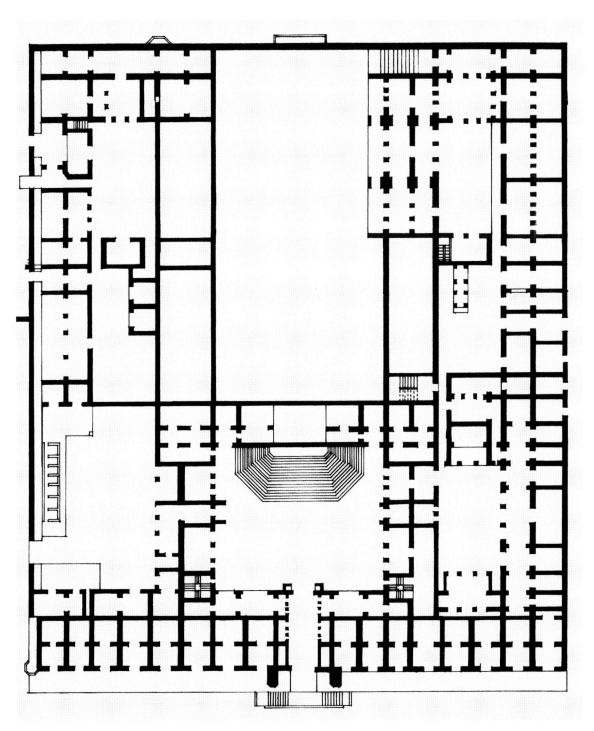

57 Plan of the Ramachandra temple at the level of the outer courtyard.

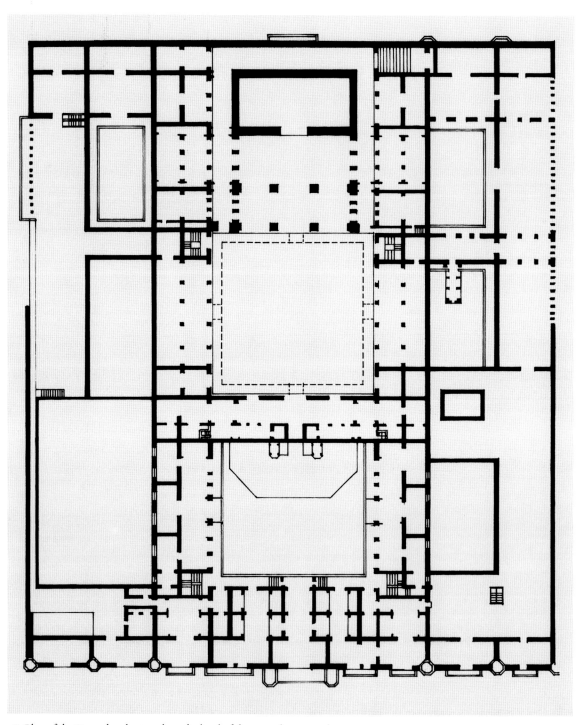

58 Plan of the Ramachandra temple at the level of the central courtyard.

place for an auspicious image of Ganesh (illus. 121).

Together the four façades, with marked and often enhanced central features, set the two central axes that intersect at the *brahmasthana*. A module of a pavilion, comprising a *bangaldar* roof unit flanked on either side by a *gumbaj* or domed *chhatri*, sits over each of the central divisions of the four façades (see, for example, illus. 62 and 63). The central *bangaldar* roof unit is further subdivided into three arched sections, with the central arch marginally wider than the other two. This re-marks the central axis not only of the *bangaldar* unit, but also of the module and the whole of the façade. Also at the roof level, in the corners of the courtyard, are further domed *chhatris* marking the ends of each side.

The centrality of the courtyard is established not only by its inherent function as an open space, but also by the sides that enclose it. The symmetry set up between the opposite sides in terms of their divisions and decorative features, the odd number of subdivisions, and the decorative and dimensional enhancement of the central division are all visual expressions of the concept of centrality. And because each side is connected conceptually with the opposite side, the centrality established on the façades is stretched into a central axis. The two central axes intersect at the centre point of the courtyard (illus. 65). This concept of centrality and axes is followed even at the micro level, in the definition of a niche, for example. The frame that defines the niche is marked by a *galat* (border) of radiating leaves that change their inclination at the central points of the sides of the frame (illus. 66). The axes are established by the points on the sides where the leaves leaning in opposite directions meet.

Beyond the sides that make the courtyard lie the covered parts of the building, such as an arcade followed by another arcade, or by a fully covered range of rooms. The layering may be physical in terms of actual space beyond, or it may be conceptual in terms of a sculpted representation of such spaces, or a combination of physical and conceptual layering may be employed in articulating the façades. In the interior of a room and on the courtyard walls of traditional buildings it is common to find a *khat* or dado panel that runs all along the surface of the wall at a height of about 1 m from the floor. The characteristic feature of a dado panel is that it is finished with an impervious plaster called *araish*, which makes it suitable for use with low furniture and to lean against. It is usually framed with bold black borders, which may be floral and colourful or plain. The panel itself is in plain white *araish*, but may also be decorated. In a traditional setting, the surface of the dado panel is in contact with the human body and is considered the uppermost surface in the rendering of the walls. All features immediately above the panel conceptually recede behind it.

On the western wall of the temple courtyard the columns of the niches recede behind the dado panel (illus. 67). This is evident in the way the *galat* of the niche immediately above the panel is articulated: it has no lower border framing the niche, suggesting its continuation; and the radiating leaves do not change their angle of inclination, suggesting that the centre points of the sides lie hidden behind the *khat*. On either side of the niches are the columns that may seem to have made way for the niches to emerge to the foreground. But actually the two half-columns that flank the door surround represent the depth of the module. It is an orthographic depiction of a projecting module, whose depth is suggested by corner columns. This constitutes the next layer of panels, framed by columns that were whole. Proceeding through the façade is the third layer of

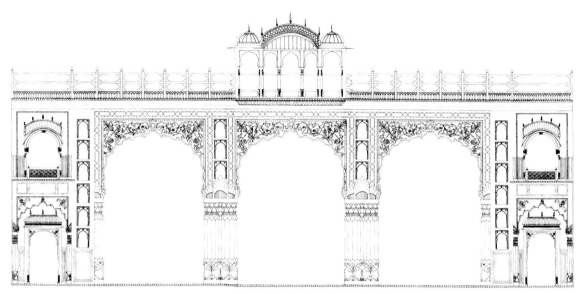

59 The east, or temple side of the central courtyard.

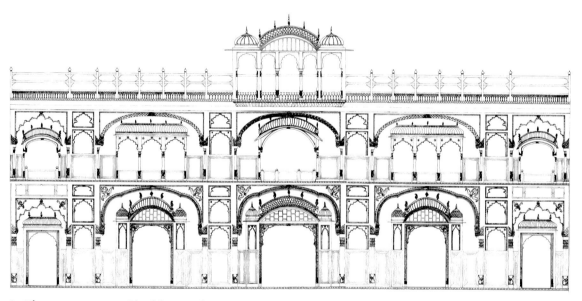

60 The west, or entrance side of the central courtyard.

61 Detail of illus. 59.

62 The temple (or eastern) side of the central courtyard.

63 The northern side of the central courtyard.

64 A corner between the northern and eastern sides of the central courtyard.

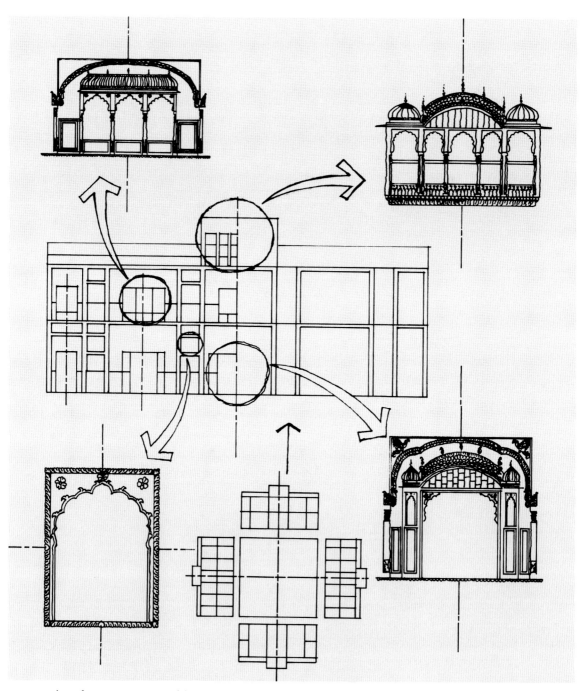

65 Centrality of axes. Lower centre: fold-out depiction of the courtyard's four sides, establishing axes that meet at the courtyard's centre. Middle: schematic depiction of the western side with (peripheries) details of some of its parts.

panels that frame the opening.

Another common example of the articulation of layering is the case of vanishing columns (illus. 122). Beyond the arcade, on the inner walls of the northern and the southern façades, is a depiction of arches and columns in relief. The columns terminate without touching the floor at the point where they meet the dado panel, to suggest their continuation behind the panel. The niches on the same wall are similarly devoid of their lower border to suggest a layer beyond the panel. Layering of all these kinds suggests a series of concentric zones, like the *vithis* (concentric zones) of the *mandala*, radiating from the centre (illus. 68).

The building is united by motifs that remain consistent throughout. The uniformity in design of architectural features such as columns is sustained even with a change of materials. Whether they are structural, in relief, or partially depicted, they are fully consistent in their design. It is common for a building to have an overriding framework of motifs, which are particular to that building. In the case of the Ramachandra Temple this is a variety of *chhatris* or roof types: *kamani* (bow) and *bangaldar* roofs in relief and on pavilions on the roof; *gumbaj* or domed roofs in relief and on the roof; and *vedi chhatri* or flattened roofs in relief. A *bangaldar* roof, when not flanked on either side by domed *chhatris*, is accompanied by a circular arch.

The cusped arch used throughout the building comprises three elements: a *chugga* or the central cusp, usually topped by a flower; *bangri* or intermediary cusps, usually odd in number on either side of the *chugga*; and a *goda* or knee, where the arch meets the top of the column (illus. 69–71). The proportion of the individual elements is geometrically constructed within the rectangle between the *galat* and the invisible line joining the tops of the columns. The courtyard also uses a

series of circular arches such as the *kamani* or the bow arch, a double-curved arch and a circular arch. Note the characteristic *goda* and the flower of the *chugga* employed in these circular arches. All these arches and their component parts, irrespective of their precise shapes, are geometrically derived from their encasing rectangles. This is so even in what seems a simple case of splitting the arch along its central cusp (illus. 70). The width is divided into five parts, of which two parts are horizontal on either side of the centre, so that the length of the horizontal element of the arch is directly proportional to the width of the opening. 'Splitting' the arch is an architectural device to keep the line of columns consistent through the elevation. Because its geometric construction does not depend on the height of its encasing rectangle (which is the case with a fully cusped arch), it allows for variation in the size of the opening while maintaining the level of horizontal markers throughout the elevation. All features follow a consistent proportioning system. For example, the shafts of columns are twice the height of their bases; the height of the openings is one and a half times or twice the width; and the height of the upper floor is a twelfth shorter than the lower floor.

At the start of this chapter we gave some examples of a style of analysis that has long prevailed, especially among architects in their interpretation of the heritage. Such analysis typically involves overlapping dualities, between the 'abstract' and the 'cultural', or between the 'physical' and the 'spiritual'. Its aim is to discern and isolate aspects of traditional architecture that can be of service in new design. But because the concerns that structure the analysis are unhistorical, the analysis itself distorts the past it seeks to reveal. Rejecting this approach, we have gone on to offer a detailed description of

66 *Galat* detail from the *Vishvakarma Prakash Darpan*.

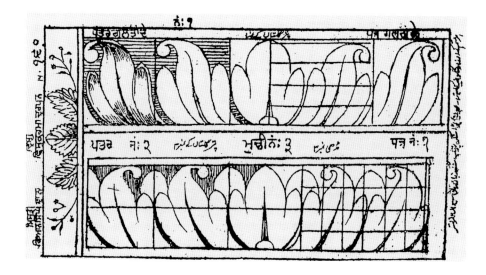

67 Layering. Half of the western range, depicted as a series of layers with the dado (bottom) outermost.

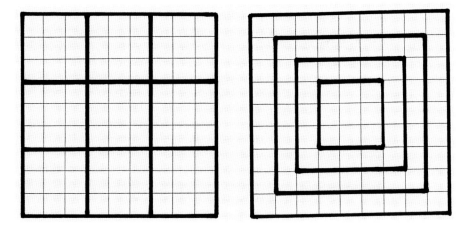

68 Two ways of seeing the *mandala*: as a mesh, and as concentric zones (*vithis*).

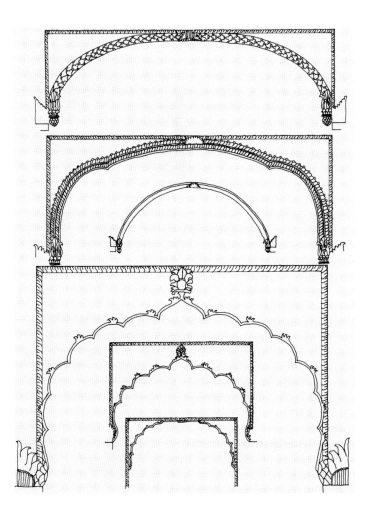

69 Varieties of arch employed in the design.

70 Arch construction
(from the *Vishvakarma
Prakash Darpan*).

71 *Goda* detail (from
the *Vishvakarma
Prakash Darpan*).

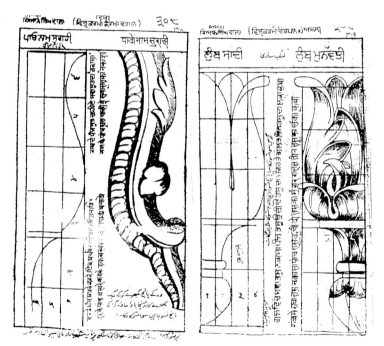

one historical building that is couched entirely in terms of the ideas and vocabulary of *vasta vidya*, the approach that prevailed at the time of its construction.

Seen in such terms, every part of the Ramachandra Temple – from the layout to the smallest detail – becomes intelligible. Throughout our analysis we have invoked ideas that are commonly expressed in *vastu shastra* texts, to show how such ideas shaped the design process of the Ramachandra Temple. We have referred to the ideas in the texts rather than quoting from the texts extensively, to avoid the 'match and test' method of architectural analysis that we have already rejected.[31] It is not that particular prescriptive passages have been selectively obeyed, but rather that *vastu vidya* as a whole provided the intellectual hinterland for the design. The texts are not inscribed on the walls. There was no need of that, for the design philosophy that they embody was already understood by designers and users alike. But this coherent philosophy began to unravel, as a result of the intervention of competing design philosophies during the British period, as we shall see.

72 The Naya Mahal, Jaipur.

4 Rules and Rulers

In 1818, like other Rajput states in western India, Jaipur entered into an alliance with the East India Company. By the terms of the treaty, Jaipur recognized the Company's sovereignty in return for a guarantee of its borders and internal autonomy.[1] The payment of a regular tribute to the Company was no doubt preferable to the more erratic extortions by the Marathas, which had characterized the preceding decades, especially as it earned the promise of protection from any such disruption in the future. The full impact of the treaty, both politically and culturally, was not felt until much later in the century. Initially, its significance was slight because the Company had comparatively less interest in the western regions. For example, as James Tod, who as political agent to the western Rajput states had helped to prepare the ground for the treaties, was nevertheless inclined to suggest – in the dedications to King George IV and to King William IV of his mammoth study of Rajput history, published in 1829–32 – Britain's interests would be best served by ensuring the Rajput states' full independence.[2] But the general refashioning of British rule under the Crown rather than the Company, following the revolt of 1857, introduced more interventionist policies. Although Rajasthan itself was superficially little involved in the events of 1857, British relations with all the Indian states were thereafter put on a more regular footing.

From this point until the dissolution of Britain's Indian empire in 1947, the arrangement was that the Maharaja swore allegiance to the Crown and in all external matters his state was directed by the imperial government or 'Raj'; but in return he was recognized as a 'Prince' and his state remained internally autonomous. He maintained his own state government or *darbar*, led by his own chief minister or *diwan*. As in the Mughal period, the members of the *darbar* and the holders of the principal offices of state were the Maharaja's clansmen, the *thakurs* or hereditary chiefs of districts (*thikanas*) within the state; however, again as before, they held no monopoly of power since other subjects of the Maharaja – and notably Muslims and Jains – were also employed in administrative capacities, and ritual posts were naturally held by Brahmins. The greatest change was the increasing influence on internal affairs of the British Resident, the representative of the Raj at the Maharaja's court. He acted as a personal guide to the Maharaja and as an advisor to his *darbar*, and his advice could not lightly be ignored. In addition, some aspects of the state's administration – especially those connected with its programme of modernization – were entrusted to European specialists, seconded from the Raj to the service of the *darbar*. So while an Indian system of government prevailed, there was a considerable measure of Western intervention.

The architecture of Jaipur state in this period reflects this balance because of the employment of selective British individual specialists in this field as in others. An Indian building system was sustained insofar as the majority of building professionals were Indian, and *vastu vidya* continued to be applied in building practice; but this approach was developed and then stretched to breaking point as a result of the introduction of Western methods in both practice and education. Particularly important in this regard was the work of the office of Samuel Swinton Jacob, a British engineer who ran the Jaipur State Public Works Department (PWD) throughout the last three decades of the nineteenth century, and who exerted considerable influence on the architecture of Jaipur and neighbouring states through this period and beyond. Ultimately destructive of local traditional methods, his intervention nevertheless sparked some moments of creative interaction. In this chapter we chart this process through a selection of public and royal buildings of the period between the 1880s and the 1930s, against the comparative background of the much greater dominance of Western methods in British India (that is, regions under direct British rule). Our account draws on the writings of the chief protagonists and the records of the relevant departments of state.

The Educational Reforms of Sawai Ram Singh II, 1835–80

British intervention in the domestic policy of Jaipur began even before the transfer of power from the East India Company to the Crown and the new per-spectives ushered in by that change. Maharaja Sawai Ram Singh II succeeded to the *gaddi* (throne) of Jaipur as a child in 1835 but did not come to power until 1854. In his youth, responsibility for the super-vision of his education was assumed by Major John Ludlow – appointed British Resident in 1844 – who

insisted on an English style of curriculum.[3] Nor did the Major neglect the Maharaja's subjects (amongst whom he was known as 'Ladoo Sahib'): in 1844, together with Pandit Shiv Deen who served as its first principal, he founded the Maharaja's College, originally a secondary school providing instruction in Sanskrit, Urdu and English. From the initial intake of 40 pupils, the College grew rapidly and in 1852 it was split to create the separate Sanskrit College under Hari Das Shastri. There was conscious emulation here of the education policies of pre-Macaulay British India: similar modern Sanskrit colleges had been founded under British patronage in Benares (1791), Poona (1821) and Calcutta (1824). In 1865 the Jaipur Sanskrit College was relocated to the complex of the Ramachandra Temple (as described in Chapter Three). The Maharaja's College was housed in another large temple building immediately facing the Hawa Mahal (illus. 73).[4] By 1875 the Maharaja's College had swollen to 800 pupils and the Sanskrit College exceeded 200. Both institutions continued to flourish in later decades, with BA degrees introduced in 1890 and higher degrees in 1896.[5]

These were just the first two of a spate of educational, cultural and welfare institutions founded during the long course of Ram Singh's reign. Others included the Rajput School, the Medical School, the Girls' School, the School of Art, the Public Library, a printing press, the Ram Prakash Theatre, a meteorological observatory and Mayo Hospital. Ram Singh reorganized the Pandit Sabha (initially founded by his ancestor, Mirza Raja Jai Singh I) to encourage discussion of social and sectarian reform amongst *pandits*, and, if this seemed to lack a secular edge, it was matched in 1859 by a Social Services Congress.[6]

Measures were also taken to clean up and modernize the by now ageing fabric of the walled

73 The Maharaja's College, on Sireh Deori Bazaar.

city. The drawbridges over the ditch outside the gates on the southern side of the city were replaced by permanent stone bridges to ease access, and the city streets were metalled and paved with stone along their centres.[7] The step-wells or *baoris* located at the two central crossroads, which had been a major source of water for the city's inhabitants, were by 1868 rendered redundant by the introduction of piped water, and, being now judged unhygienic, were filled in. They were later replaced by gardens with fountains (illus. 74).[8] All of this was well in line with British policy for the Indian states: it was just the sort of development that it was part of the Resident's function to encourage. And Ram Singh's efforts were duly acknowledged by

British patronage. In 1869 he was made a member of the Legislative Council of India, and in 1877 (three years before his death) he became a member of the Privy Council.[9]

Before examining how this changing social and educational climate affected architecture, one of these new institutions deserves a slightly closer inspection. The School of Art was opened by the Maharaja in 1866. Art schools had been established in the Presidency towns of British India (Calcutta, Madras and Bombay) and in Lahore in the preceding decade, and obviously to some extent they were the inspiration; but while the curricula of those schools initially centred on Western drawing styles, the Jaipur school – at the express wish of the

74 View of Bari Chopar by Raja Deen Dayal (1876), showing the step-well, partly enclosed.

darbar – departed from that model: it was a school not of fine art but of industrial design.[10] The curriculum certainly included drawing and skills of Western origin, such as clock-making and electroplating, but most of the subjects taught related to local traditional crafts. They included carpentry and wood-carving, clay modelling and pottery (imported from Khurja), stone sculpture, filigree work, blacksmithing, *koft-gari* (inlaying gold on steel), embroidery and engraving (illus. 75).[11] Instruction was given free to sons of the artisan class. Courses lasted from three to five years and were intended to impart 'a sound practical education in those Industrial arts' which would secure employment for the graduates.[12] The number of such pupils exceeded 100 by 1877 and rose to over 150 in the second decade of the twentieth century.[13]

In its early years the direction of the school was entrusted to a member of the small coterie of European professionals seconded to the state to help in the implementation of the *darbar*'s programme of modernization. Surgeon Major F. W. de Fabeck was not, in fact, a professional art educator but a physician and his principal duties lay in that domain. But like some of his European colleagues in Jaipur he devoted his leisure hours to other, more artistic, pursuits. He was, for example,

75 Pottery made at the School of Art (from Hendley, 1884).

76 Mayo Hospital, designed by F. W. de Fabeck, 1870–75.

not only the surgeon but also the architect of the Mayo Hospital (built 1870–75; illus. 76).[14] The purpose of the school – the revival of local industrial design – was established under his direction and pursued by his successor (from 1875 to 1907), Opendro Nath Sen. Other important early personnel included 'Luchman' (Lakhshman), the original drawing master; his younger brother and successor Ram Baksh, who had been a pupil of the school; and the star graduate of their department, Jai Chand, who was one of many to find appropriate employment, in his case in the office of the state's Executive Engineer. That it is the names of the drawing masters – rather than, say, the wood-carvers – that are recorded in the school's reports reflects perhaps the influence of Western values; and Ram Baksh was particularly commended for introducing drawing from nature; but at the same time the reports emphasize the importance and the success of 'mechanical skill and handiwork'.[15]

The Jaipur Exhibition and Museum, 1880–84

The next major step in the resurgence of the arts in Jaipur was the exhibition of 1883, displaying products of the School of Art and comparable recent work from other parts of India. Again there was a colonial model: the precursor of this, as of the many other exhibitions of industrial art held in the period, was the Great Exhibition of 1851, though few of those which followed could rival the original's scale. The Jaipur Exhibition coincided with the Calcutta International Exhibition of 1883–4, and was the first major such event to be held in an Indian state.

The new Maharaja, Sawai Madho Singh II (r. 1880–1922), began to assemble objects in 1881 and

these were continuously displayed in a small improvised museum. In 1883 the completion of a new palace administrative building on the eastern side of Jaleb Chowk, the outer courtyard of the palace bordering Sireh Deori Bazaar, provided the occasion for this display to be relocated and promoted as a special temporary (two-month) exhibition. The building, known as the Naya Mahal, was designed in a neo-classical style by the Executive Engineer, Samuel Swinton Jacob.[16] Additional objects were loaned for the display by the Maharajas of neighbouring states. The purpose of the exhibition, as later recalled by its organizer – another surgeon, Thomas Holbein Hendley – was not simply to entertain the public but more importantly 'to present to the craftsmen selected examples of the best works of India, in the hope that they would profit thereby'.[17] Like de Fabeck before him, Hendley was concerned to promote indigenous skills and he believed that this meant discouraging the Westernization of design. Although his main role in Jaipur was to assist in a process of modernization, including the spread of Western medicine, he shared the view of some other arts revivalists of the period that as far as design was concerned progress could come only through the delivery from Western involvement and that – somewhat paradoxically – he could assist here too. Thus most of the objects in the exhibition he considered 'worthy of imitation', but he deliberately included a few works 'which show what should have been avoided, and what mischief has already been done by the contact between Oriental and European art'.[18]

Prizes for the best works were awarded by a board of jurors that included the leading arts educator John Lockwood Kipling. Seen by over a quarter of a million people,[19] the exhibition was later commemorated in a magnificent four-volume work prepared by Hendley and sponsored by the Maharaja.[20] Apart from the objects in the exhibition, this book also reproduced the paintings from the celebrated *Razmnama*, the Persian version of the *Mahabharata* that had been prepared for the Emperor Akbar, and had been acquired from the imperial library by Sawai Jai Singh. On the strength of this exhibition, Jaipur became a major contributor to the London Colonial and Indian Exhibition of 1886, when all of the local skills – stonework, pottery, jewellery, enamelling, metalwork, lacquer and textiles – were again represented, along with anthropological and mythological items.[21]

From the exhibitions, the next logical step was the creation of a permanent public museum with the same objective. Such an institution had in fact been conceived back in 1876, during the reign of Ram Singh. Indeed, when the Prince of Wales visited Jaipur in February of that year he laid the foundation-stone of a building to be known, after himself, as the Albert Hall.[22] Plans at this early stage were vague: there was little idea as to the building's contents and no design had been prepared. The following year, an advertisement invited competitive designs and 27 entries were submitted to the Maharaja. None of these, however, was deemed suitable, and the Maharaja turned instead to de Fabeck,[23] no doubt encouraged by his success in designing the Hospital, which had been opened by (and named after) the Viceroy, Lord Mayo, when he visited Jaipur in December 1875. De Fabeck had also designed the state's boarding-house in the grounds of Mayo College in Ajmer, in 1873–6.[24] But the Maharaja was to be disappointed. In 1879 de Fabeck received 'a letter and remuneration from the Maharaja', who handed the matter over to the *darbar*.[25] The death of the Maharaja on 18 September 1880 was a further

distraction from progress, and the *darbar* then asked Swinton Jacob to superintend the work.[26]

Samuel Swinton Jacob was born in 1841 into a distinguished military family.[27] He first joined the Royal Artillery, transferred to the Indian Army and then trained as an engineer in the Public Works Department of British India. In 1867 he was appointed Executive Engineer in Jaipur, taking over a fledgling state public works department that had been founded in 1860, on the British model.[28] This department was staffed with local craftsmen and draughtsmen including graduates from the School of Art. Its major work was not the design of great public buildings but the construction of roads and canals. Its architectural projects were mostly utilitarian and uninspiring: in a typical year the department constructed outhouses for the hospital, a guard house for the Residency and a compound wall around the post office.[29]

Jacob differed from many of his former colleagues in the British PWD in taking a more modest view of the architectural capacities of an engineer such as himself, unassisted. For example, when writing a report on the progress of de Fabeck's Mayo Hospital in 1872 – a building to which Jacob contributed as engineer – he suggested that the model it offered of co-operation between engineer and architect held lessons for the PWD: 'there is no doubt that it would be of immense benefit.'[30] He was further distinguished by his respect for local building traditions; and in the case of the Albert Hall he turned not to another European but to his colleagues in his department for that co-operation. As is recorded in an inscription on its facade, the design and construction of the Albert Hall was a collaborative project between Jacob as 'superintendent' and Mir Tujumoul Hoosein, an overseer within the department, who acted as 'supervisor'. They were assisted by the draughtsmen Ram Baksh, Shankar Lal and Chote Lal, and by the *mistris* (masons) Chander and Tara.

These were merely the team leaders. At the height of the construction process, during 1883 and 1884, according to the state PWD's annual reports, the workforce included nearly 50 masons, between three and four times that number of stonecutters, over 100 *beldars* (less skilled stoneworkers and specialists in cement), 68 *coolies* (porters) and eight stone polishers.[31] The distinctions made in these lists reflect more than the various specialisms required within a workforce; they indicate also the continuation of the indigenous approach to building construction. As against a post-Renaissance European method, by which a single designer–architect determines the overall design and its detailing on paper before handing it to the building specialists to execute, the pre-modern Indian system was more collaborative, and the responsibility for design was shared. Thus the 50 or so 'masons' who executed the detailed stonework on the Albert Hall also determined what they were carving; they were the designers of the motifs they made. This fact is made explicit by a comment of Jacob's: writing of the building later, he observed that the masons had examined 'old buildings near Delhi and Agra and elsewhere. In some cases designs have been followed, or have inspired the workmen here.'[32] If the masons were not also designers, then their sources of inspiration would not have been an issue. And the point is reinforced by Hendley, curator of the exhibition, who noted that the draughtsmen spent months studying buildings in Delhi and Fatehpur Sikri and subsequently made 'good designs, which are not copies of those originals, but really new creations of the same school.'[33]

This study of Mughal – and of Rajput –

monuments was actively encouraged by Jacob.[34] The craftsmen produced scale drawings of building elements, from larger parts such as *chhatris* and *jharokhas* (projecting windows) and column types, to small details such as brackets and plinth mouldings, and these drawings could subsequently be used as models or inspiration for their new designs (illus. 77). Later Jacob went further. In an effort to promote this method beyond the borders of Jaipur and to make the drawings equally available to masons elsewhere, he published them as the celebrated *Jaipur Portfolio*. The first six volumes of this massive work were printed by Bernard Quaritch in 1890, under the patronage of the Maharaja, Madho Singh. A further six volumes, printed by Griggs & Sons, were issued between 1894 and 1913. Besides the historical examples, the later volumes also include some drawings of designs that had been produced within Jacob's office, presumably to demonstrate the method in process. These are carefully labelled as to their origin. But one drawing of a conspicuous component of the Albert Hall is also included without being so designated – evidence again that the details of this building were produced to designs by people other than Jacob himself (illus. 78).[35]

On the face of it then, the intervention into public building in Jaipur of a British PWD-trained engineer did not result in any marked change in method. The design team was assembled, and to a considerable degree educated, by Jacob, but the terms of their engagement with each other and with the building process sustained the method that had produced all of the earlier buildings in the state, a method not displaced but augmented by the addition of Jacob.

But when we turn from the process to the product – to the built form itself – we find that the ideas introduced by this new team member certainly

77 Details of a bracket from a temple in Jaipur, from the *Jaipur Portfolio*.

78 Elevation and section of a *chhatri* of the Albert Hall, from the *Jaipur Portfolio*.

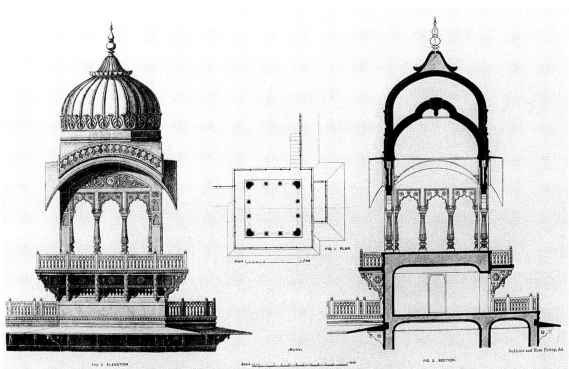

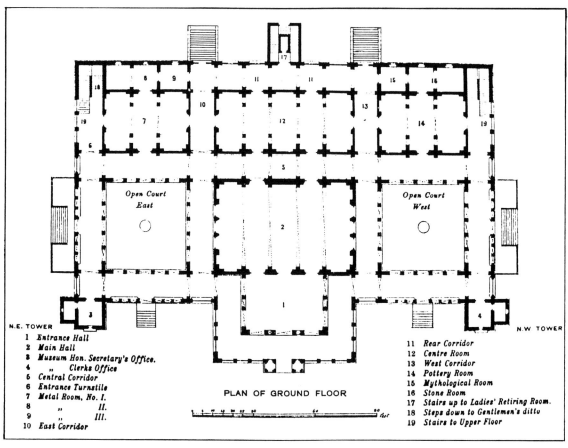

PLAN OF GROUND FLOOR

1 Entrance Hall
2 Main Hall
3 Museum Hon. Secretary's Office.
4 „   Clerks Office
5 Central Corridor
6 Entrance Turnstile
7 Metal Room, No. I.
8 „   II.
9 „   III.
10 East Corridor

11 Rear Corridor
12 Centre Room
13 West Corridor
14 Pottery Room
15 Mythological Room
16 Stone Room
17 Stairs up to Ladies' Retiring Room.
18 Steps down to Gentlemen's ditto
19 Stairs to Upper Floor

N.E. TOWER

N.W TOWER

Open Court East

Open Court West

79 Plan of the ground floor of the Albert Hall.

had an impact on the *vidya*, the logic by which the building was composed. This is most apparent from the plan (illus. 79). The rear half of the building comprises three long galleries of double height, arranged in a row, and together providing the main exhibition space. The galleries are surrounded by corridors. Centrally placed in front of them is a spacious hall intended for lectures and public meetings,[36] flanked on either side by an open courtyard. As we have seen, the older Mughal and Rajput architecture of the region provided the models for the building's stonework. That the plan type has no such relationship with these traditions is perhaps not surprising: as a museum, the building functionally marks a departure from those traditions, and in creating a European style of institution in Jaipur, Jacob (we may surmise) has relied rather on European planning models for the general layout. It could be said that this marks rather more than an expansion of the Jaipur builders' *vastu vidya*: in some respects it completely displaces it. For example, the placing of open courtyards near the margins of the plan, to flank a covered space, inverts the established method of placing courtyards internally, to be surrounded by covered spaces or *shalas*, as in the Ramachandra Temple.

80 The Albert Hall (City Museum), Jaipur, 1880–87.

The external massing of the building, though logically related to the plan, remarkably exhibits much less divergence from conventional forms (illus. 80). Indeed, the stepped pyramid effect, with the recession of storeys upwards, is very unlike any European museum prototype and does recall precedents within the Mughal–Rajput traditions, from minor pavilions such as the Panch Mahal at Fatehpur Sikri to palace structures such as those at Orchha, and – most obviously and most relevantly – the City Palace in Jaipur itself. Furthermore, those traditions are developed by the building's carefully designed and exquisitely executed details, particularly of the exterior (illus. 123). As Hendley noted, these are no mere copies from historic monuments grafted onto the facades; they are original solutions, which contribute to an integrated design.

Jacob aimed to revive and advance, and so demonstrate the viability of, local building traditions. His openness to collaboration ensured the continuance of the indigenous process and secured a partial success, especially in those details left wholly to his colleagues. But the abandonment of established compositional convention means that, in its larger parts, the building does not sustain central elements of the indigenous *vastu vidya*. From his silence on the subject – his lack of reference, for example, to any text – it seems reasonable to infer that Jacob was wholly unaware of *vastu vidya*, that is, of the knowledge base of the tradition he sought to sustain. He thought of that tradition in terms of craft skills; ironically the consequence of his intervention was therefore the beginning of the unravelling of the tradition, and in particular the separation of the ornamental parts of design from their wider conceptual context.

The Museum was formally opened in 1887 and was 'open without admission charge, to visitors of all classes, between dawn and dusk on weekdays'.[37] What those visitors would see, chiefly, were the objects of the 1883 exhibition, now provided with a permanent home. Some that had been provided by neighbouring states were now purchased.[38] The Museum carried forward the exhibition's didactic purposes, to inform the public and to offer models to craftsmen, and this education continued to be under strict guidance. For example, some European objects were also acquired for comparative purposes but 'no European forms are allowed to be copied, [while] all good specimens of Indian artwork are freely lent to the local workmen for reproduction'.[39]

The fabric of the building itself contributed to this end by representing the architectural skills that could not be accommodated within the displays. As Jacob put it, 'the endeavour has been to make the walls themselves a Museum, by taking advantage of many of the beautiful designs in old buildings near Delhi and Agra and elsewhere.'[40] Or, as Hendley explained, 'Jeypore has always been famous throughout North India for the beauty of its carving in stone; but as the architect relied upon this feature for the chief ornamentation of his building, it has not been thought necessary to illustrate this local art, but rather to direct the visitor's attention to the principal decorative examples in the edifice itself.'[41] Again, what these comments imply is a separation of the decorative elements from the larger structure, the fragmentation of a formerly cohesive tradition.[42] The Museum building was to be seen by architectural craftsmen as a sort of three-dimensional *Jaipur Portfolio*.

The Public Works Department and the Indo-Saracenic Movement

> The [British] Indian Public Works Department, as a body, has not hitherto been successful in its architectural efforts, and all who know what vast stores of material lie scattered over the land, must regret the poverty of design and detail which, as a rule, characterizes modern buildings in this country . . . Standard plans are too often produced, and buildings are erected by men who have no sympathy with Oriental architecture . . .[43]

In publicizing the work of his own department, Jacob intended a criticism of the larger body on which it was modelled, the Public Works Department of British India. In view of our reservations about his success, it is worth comparing his work with what was happening at the same time in British India, where the balance of power was somewhat different. Briefly then, we must shift our focus away from Jaipur towards the much larger territories under direct British rule.

Established in 1854 by the Governor General Lord Dalhousie, the PWD was responsible for communication systems such as roads, canals and the telegraph, and for all public buildings. This last category was immensely broad: it included churches, town halls, high courts, museums and other such grand public institutions in the cities; but it also included every civilian and military officer's bungalow, every small district court house, police station and school room, every chapel and collector's office, in every town and district throughout the length and breadth of British India. The sheer quantity of work was thus enormous: the remit of the PWD covered nothing less than the entire infrastructure of a growing empire.

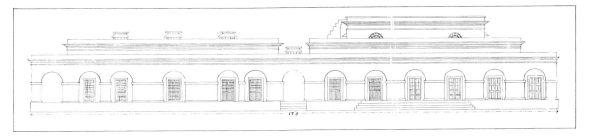

81 Architecture according to the PWD Standard Plans; from Kipling 1886.

82 The PWD classical mode: a bungalow in Agra.

It might be supposed that the pressing need for so many buildings of so many types so rapidly presented great opportunities for talented architects to flourish. Not so. With respect to all the lesser and provincial works in this catalogue – numerically the majority – the prevailing ethos of the PWD was utilitarian. Indian builders were employed in junior posts, but only after they had been retrained in Western engineering at the government college in Roorkee, and they were not permitted to bring to their work anything of their own traditions. The solution to the problem of quantity offered by the PWD was the Standard Plans, predetermined designs for each of the various types of building, many of which had a basic common denominator. The Standard Plans offered multi-purpose bungalows, and the design process was reduced to the minimal modification required to fit the building to the place and need (illus. 81 and 82). An order of 1864 forbade deviation from these plans, which were generally in a stripped and functional classicist style. No Indian element was tolerated and no use of indigenous craftsmanship was admitted; and as a result they became the particular target of criticism from Jacob and others.[44]

At the more prestigious end of the architectural spectrum in the cities, the Standard Plans did not apply and a greater pluralism gradually developed.

Before the mid-nineteenth century, to be sure, British buildings were almost uniformly in Western classical styles. They were designed mostly by military engineers, using pattern books and published plans by leading British architects. A prominent early example is Government House in Calcutta, built between 1799 and 1803, to a design prepared by Lieutenant Charles Wyatt, based on the plan for Kedleston Hall that had been published by James Paine in 1783 (illus. 83). By the time the PWD was founded, the hegemony of classicism was already being challenged by the Gothic. An early example

83 Government House, Calcutta, by Charles Wyatt, 1799–1803.

84 Tropical Gothic: a detail of the Taj Mahal Hotel, Bombay,
by W. Chambers, *c.* 1900.

85 The Law Courts, Madras, by J. W. Brassington and Henry Irwin, 1888–92.

is St Paul's Cathedral in Calcutta, designed by Major W. N. Forbes in 1839. But the Gothic took wing with the development of Bombay in the 1860s and '70s, initiated under the governorship of Sir Bartle Frere (1862–7) and continued notably in the construction of the University Convocation Hall and Library (1869–78) to designs supplied by George Gilbert Scott, and in the somewhat eclectic Victoria Terminus (1878–87) by F. W. Stevens. A late addition was the world-renowned Taj Mahal Hotel by W. Chambers (1900; illus. 84).

From the 1870s this stylistic pluralism opened up a major debate amongst architects and political leaders about the desirability of adopting a single architectural style as the official imagery of the British Raj, and about what that style should be. To dismiss this debate as an irrelevance on the ground that it addressed merely the superficial matter of style would, of course, be to apply to the nineteenth century a peculiarly twentieth-century perspective, and to miss a crucial point: to those who participated in the debate, style was a central concern, and this emphasis was germane to the impact of Western thought on Indian architecture in the colonial period. Broadly, the debate reflected the famous battle of the styles that raged in Victorian Britain, but in the Indian context it had a special focus as the style adopted would communicate the core purpose of British rule. Classicism, being associated with a Western rationalist tradition, and

86 The Gateway of India, Bombay, by George Wittet, 1911.

Gothic, identified as Christian, implied different essential values, and so expressed divergent ideas about the mission of a paternalistic Raj.

On the other hand, both styles were self-consciously foreign in an Indian context, and presented to British eyes images of 'ourselves', however that was construed. A third possible approach was considered more assimilationist: the adoption of Indian historical styles, or of a form of architecture more or less closely derived from them, might be seen to impart an Indian character to British rule. This approach was dubbed 'Indo-Saracenic'. Its early political supporters included Lord Napier, Governor of Madras, while early practitioners included his consulting architect R. F. Chisholm, who designed the University Senate House and Board of Revenue offices in the city in the 1870s. The vogue was sustained by his successors in office, J. W. Brassington and Henry Irwin, who share responsibility for the Madras Law Courts (1888–92; illus. 85). Other early practitioners include William Emerson, who designed Muir College in Allahabad in 1870, and Charles Mant, who designed the main building of Mayo College in Ajmer in 1875. Bombay converted from Gothic to Indo-Saracenic in the Edwardian era, with the General Post Office of John Begg (1904–10) and the Prince of Wales Museum and the Gateway of India by George Wittet (1908–15; illus. 86).

87 Laxmi Vilas, Baroda, by Charles Mant, 1878–90.

All of these cities lay in British India, but the Indo-Saracenic movement was not limited to that sphere. A pseudo-Indian style in the hands of British architect–engineers, it appealed also to some of the Maharajas of Indian states who were deemed 'progressive'. Some had willingly embraced Western styles, and especially classicism; but while this implied a cultural reorientation towards the central power, it tended also to open a schism between the Maharaja and the majority of his subjects. The Indo-Saracenic movement offered a solution to this dilemma: it enabled a Maharaja at once to keep pace with imperial building policies and to keep a trace of the indigenous heritage. Major patrons included the Maharaja of

Travancore, who employed Chisholm to design a Museum in 1872; the Maharaja of Baroda, who employed Mant to design (and Chisholm to complete) a vast new palace, Laxmi Vilas (1878–90; illus. 87); and the Maharaja of Mysore, who employed Irwin to design another palace, the Amba Vilas, in 1900. In the early twentieth century the Nizam of Hyderabad employed Vincent Esch to design numerous public buildings, including the High Court and Osmania Hospital (illus. 88).

Much has been written about the Indo-Saracenic movement elsewhere, with varying analyses, and it is unnecessary to repeat the arguments here.[45] We have introduced it here to establish a wider context for developments in Jaipur, and to

88 The High Court, Hyderabad, by Vincent Esch, 1916; photograph by the architect.

make two major points in our argument.

The first relates to knowledge. Amongst these Indo-Saracenic designs the degree of fidelity to Indian models is very diverse. Some are eclectic, mixing elements from widely divergent sources, while in other cases the stated aim was to adhere closely to a specified Indian model. In the latter category are Chisholm's art gallery in Trivandrum, which uses roof forms derived from the vernacular architecture of Kerala, and Irwin's art gallery in Madras (1907), whose details are borrowed from the (somewhat more remote) Mughal complex at Fatehpur Sikri. Similarly, Mant's Mayo College (illus. 89) was intended as a pastiche of Rajput palaces (the familiar domain of the princely pupils),

and Esch's buildings in Hyderabad adopt a characteristically Deccani sultanate vocabulary. Nevertheless, even in these cases, the architects have imitated only details of the originals; selected forms or motifs are treated as decorative embellishments on buildings that – in terms of their organization – are Western. There has been no attempt to imitate the logic of the originals, the system by which these elements were combined. In short, there is same separation of detail from structure – of form from *vidya* – that we found in Jaipur's Albert Hall. Indeed the gulf here is wider. The massing of Laxmi Vilas in Baroda, for example, is dramatic and impressive, but it owes nothing to any Gujarati – or any other Indian –

89 Mayo College, Ajmer, by Charles Mant, 1875.

prototype. The palace is an English country house got up in Indian fancy dress (illus. 87).

The second point concerns agency. The architects of all these Indo-Saracenic concoctions were British. It is true that they relied heavily on skilled Indian masons – but only to execute the details, not to design them. Mant's ability to manipulate a wide range of Indian motifs arose not from a close collaboration with Indian colleagues but from patient study: he toured, he sketched, he photographed; then he designed; and then, and only then, he called in the craftsmen to carve.[46] In public lectures Chisholm trumpeted loudly the skills of these craftsmen, and declared how much he relied on them, so that some have supposed that the hand they had in his work was a designer's one. Not so, accord-

ing to Chisholm's own testimony: he was insisting on the need to co-operate with craftsmen only 'when the design is completed'.[47] Esch similarly made a routine genuflection to the skill of his workmen; but his surviving working drawings reveal that all the details were previously worked out on paper, by himself.[48] And so here is a major point of distinction from Jaipur. In British India, and in those Indian states where the Indo-Saracenic approach was introduced, there was a considerable dependency on Indian builders, but they were not admitted as colleagues; and the design process followed the prevalent European, not the Indian method. In this context, what Jacob was attempting in Jaipur – whatever the shortcomings of the results – was truly radical. To that experiment we may now return.

Jacob's Office, 1884–1902

Jacob's collaboration on the Albert Hall necessitated a considerable expansion of his office staff. In 1884 he worked with two assistant engineers (Ghasi Ram and Rup Chand), nine overseers (including Tujumul Hoosein) and seven others (including Chiman Lal, who was later to emerge as a prominent Jaipur architect).[49] Between this period and Jacob's effective retirement in 1902, this establishment was sustained by an ever-increasing architectural workload as commissions poured in. Beyond their customary official work for Jaipur State, the office undertook projects outside, notably in other Indian states in Rajputana, and some in British India. A survey of some of these will reveal how the ideas and methods embodied in the Albert Hall were developed over the next two decades, and how they continued to undermine the *vastu vidya* base of local design.

Before this phase, Jacob's architectural efforts had been few and modest, since his energies were mainly focused on roads and irrigation. In the 1870s, under Maharaja Sawai Ram Singh, he undertook some minor building works, such as the repair of the city wall in 1872,[50] but more ambitious projects were then considered beyond the remit of his department. The few large projects of that period, such as the design of the Mayo Hospital and of the state's boarding-house at Mayo College in Ajmer, were entrusted, as we have seen, to de Fabeck, acting as a freelance. A minor exception is All Saints' Church, built in 1875–6 to designs by Jacob, a rather grim little essay in early English Gothic whose style was suggested presumably by its Anglican denomination.[51]

De Fabeck's failure to satisfy the Maharaja with his proposed design for the museum, and the accession of Maharaja Sawai Madho Singh in 1880, led to a greater involvement by Jacob's office in architectural works. There is evidence that by 1883 they were engaged on minor work within the Chandra Mahal of the palace,[52] and this is significant because such work would normally have been the responsibility of a quite distinct department of state, namely the Raj Imarat (or 'King's Buildings'). More remarkable still, in the following year the office produced the design for the *chhatri* or cenotaph of the late Maharaja, Ram Singh. When they died, the Maharajas of Jaipur were cremated at Gaitor, outside the city wall to the north. Following Rajput custom, the place of cremation is marked in each case by a pavilion or *chhatri*. Jacob's office prepared three designs, each with a corresponding plaster model.[53] The design that was selected is a close replica of the *chhatri* of Sawai Jai Singh. Originally the founder's *chhatri* stood alone, in the centre of a square platform, which was now extended northwards, to double its size, to accommodate Ram Singh's identical *chhatri* in a symmetrical composition (illus. 124).[54] The emphatic association of Ram Singh with the founder reflects the *darbar*'s view of his contribution to the state, a view that was echoed in Jacob's personal tribute: 'Surrounded as he was by many influences, some at least of which were opposed to all progress, it reflects immortal credit on his name, that he should have identified himself so consistently with the progress of civilization.'[55] Apparently nobody saw a contradiction in commemorating such a stance with a *chhatri* based on a model from over a century before.

A small project, the *chhatri* was swiftly completed. The Albert Hall, though substantially built by 1885, continued to occupy the office until the end of the decade.[56] And as it was highly visible, it began to attract other commissions. One of these was the Jubilee Buildings or Court Offices in Jodhpur, perhaps planned as early as 1887 (it was

90 Jubilee Buildings, Jodhpur; by the office of Swinton Jacob, 1887–96.

named in honour of Queen Victoria's Golden Jubilee) but built in 1893–6 (illus. 90). Working in another Indian state, the office adopted the same procedure, collaborating closely with local craftsmen; indeed the building is one of those cited in a later polemical work by Gordon Sanderson, advocating this approach.[57] The main rooms are contained in two wings on either side of a central open hall, while further ranges to the north and south extend the line of building. The planning is picturesque and suggests the hand of Jacob, but the fine stone detailing is the mark of local designers, especially as it relates closely to the palace apartments in the nearby fort of Mehrangarh.

The commission from Jodhpur was supplemented in 1895 by a further project, for a house for the Maharaja at Mount Abu, the hill station in southern Rajasthan that was both a summer retreat and a centre of pilgrimage, because of the famous medieval Jain temples at Dilwara. In the previous two years, Jacob's office had supplied plans for similar houses for the Maharaja of Jaipur and the Maharaja of Bikaner.[58] By now the office was in effect a busy architectural practice. During this same period, in addition to the work in Mount Abu, the office supplied designs for the State Bank in Madras, for a church in Ajmer and for a jail in Kishangarh.[59]

The most substantial project of this time, however, was an entire new palace, the Umed Bhawan, for the Maharaja of Kota, Umed Singh II (r. 1889–1940; illus. 91). First designed in 1894, it

91 Umed Bhawan, Kota, by the office of Swinton Jacob, 1894–5.

was expanded during the course of construction in 1895 as a result of an increased demand from the patron.[60] The consequence is a vast and complex congeries of ranges around courtyards, with no overall symmetry or coherence. Its highlight, apart from the trademark fine detailing, is a splendid Durbar Hall of traditional conception. Recently converted into a hotel, the building was not improved by alterations to its interior design made in the 1930s.

The niche in the office's work schedule occupied by the Kota palace was immediately taken up in 1896 by a still larger palace commission, the Lallgarh for the Maharaja of Bikaner, Ganga Singh (*r.* 1887–1943).[61] Ganga Singh had come to the throne as a minor and at the time of the commission he had only recently completed his schooling at Mayo College, and had not yet assumed full powers; and so it might be a mistake to suppose a strong role in the selection of the design team on his part rather than that of his *darbar* and his British advisors. In some respects Lallgarh follows the pattern of the progressive Maharaja's home, established in recent decades by new palaces such as the Jai Vilas at Gwalior, designed in 1874 by Sir Michael Filose for Maharaja Jayaji Rao Scindia (*r.* 1843–86), or the Laxmi Vilas at Baroda, designed in 1878 by Charles Mant for Maharaja Sayaji Rao III. Though diverse in style – the first example is classical Baroque, the latter is an Indo-Saracenic extravaganza – all such palaces had much in common, most notably the spacious rooms arranged on a European plan. Equipped with banquet halls, billiard rooms and even ballrooms, they offered the new Maharajas a very different lifestyle from that sustained by the fortified retreats that were constructed by their ancestors. In the very same year that Lallgarh was commissioned, R. F. Chisholm told an audience at the Royal Institute of British Architects in London that: 'It must be kept in view that the native Rajas and chiefs of India are passing through a transitional period; that an old palace like that of Ambur would be about as useless to the present Gaekwar of Baroda as to an ordinary English gentleman.'[62] In the case of Bikaner, by this logic, Lallgarh offered an escape from the cramped and castellated apartments of Junagadh, the old fort in the heart of the city, begun in the fifteenth century by the state's founder.

Ganga Singh was indeed to become, in British eyes, the paragon of a modern maharaja, a reformer of the institutions and infrastructure of his state and a contributor to the political processes and assemblies of his day. He served, for example, as first Chancellor of the Chamber of Princes, and he represented the Indian princes at the League of Nations, while at home he developed education, medicine and new communication systems. It was by no means inconsistent with this image – though equally a reminder that he was, after all, a Rajput king – that he was also an active and successful soldier. In support of his imperial masters, he fought in the First World War in France and in Egypt, at the end of which he was the Indian signatory of the Treaty of Versailles. And in the Second World War, although turning sixty, he again visited the front, in the Middle East.[63]

The four wings of Lallgarh, which together frame a large central *charbagh* style garden, were built piecemeal over a quarter of a century (illus. 92 and 93). The first main wing was completed in 1902, the second in 1912 and the last two only in 1924–6.[64] This implies a continuing commitment to the project on the part of the Maharaja as he grew into his role. But it should be noted that over the same period he also added very extensively to the range of palaces within the old fort of Junagadh (illus. 94). The whole of the eastern end of the range, from the Vikram Vilas to the Ganga Niwas (constituting in size almost half of the whole) was his work;[65] and the inclusion of a private study and drawing room over the Tripolia Gate, and of the immense Darbar Hall, suggests that he preferred this location for official and ceremonial activities – as, for example, for the celebration of his Golden Jubilee in 1937. Lallgarh, then, did not, as Chisholm and others imagined of such palaces, replace the old fort. It served a different function. Lallgarh was a residence, a private retreat; Junagadh remained the official and public court of a warrior king.

In planning and initiating the construction of Lallgarh, Jacob's office adopted their by now standard procedure, involving local builders within the design team.[66] The procedure can be discerned in the product. The details are visibly the work of local designers: no fanciful and eclectic mélange of disparate Indian motifs ripped from the pages of James Fergusson's textbook, as on many Indo-Saracenic palaces, the details here follow and develop a recognizably Bikaneri idiom of the Rajput style, closely reminiscent of the older courtyards of Junagadh. The plan, as already suggested, owes much to Western models, especially in the generous proportions of the rooms, which are a world away from the narrow galleries and intimate apartments of Junagadh. But, as we have also suggested, this is a necessary response to a changing function, the demand for a different kind of residence. And indigenous conceptions are reflected in some aspects of the plan, such as the relationship of the

92 Lallgarh, Bikaner, by the office of Swinton Jacob, 1896–1902 and later.

93 Lallgarh, the *porte-cochère* on the south front.

94 Junagadh, Bikaner, from the east, showing the upper part of the new Darbar Hall.

ranges to the internal courtyards, through verandas. So while Jacob certainly did not formulate the general layout of the palace within the intellectual framework of *vastu vidya*, nevertheless through the knowledge of his collaborators and through the imitation of prototypes, some of the habits of that system have been sustained.

Lallgarh and the other projects undertaken by Jacob's office in the neighbouring states stand in contrast not only to the Indo-Saracenic essays of Mant and Chisholm and others, but even to their own works within British India. For, while these projects were advancing, the department also produced designs for British clients, including the imperial government. The State Bank of Madras (1895) has already been mentioned. Two earlier projects, both

educational institutions, are the Senate House and other administrative buildings of the University of Allahabad (1887; illus. 95)[67] and the original building of St Stephen's College, Delhi, sponsored by the Cambridge Mission (1894).[68] Working for British India rather than for a Maharaja, the office was not at liberty in these projects to follow their normal system and engage local craftsmen, and the buildings are consequently standard – indeed somewhat pedestrian – exercises in the British Indo-Saracenic mode. A slightly later product was the Secretariat Office in Simla, designed in 1901,[69] in which the trademark Rajput idiom was abandoned altogether in favour of a Scottish baronial style, in keeping with the Viceregal Lodge, designed by Henry Irwin in 1888.

95 University Buildings, Allahabad, by the office of Swinton Jacob, 1887.

The Raj Imarat, 1900–40

On 1 April 1902, at the request of the *darbar*, Jacob (who by now had received a knighthood) was seconded to special duties in connection with the Maharaja's planned visit to Britain for the coronation of King Edward VII. His post as Superintending Engineer was filled in his absence by his deputy, C. E. Stotherd, who had joined the Jaipur PWD in 1896.[70] Subsequently, Jacob was employed for two years by the government of British India as a consultant on irrigation throughout Rajputana; and by the time he returned to Jaipur at the end of 1905, after a spell of leave in Kashmir, he decided not to resume his post, preferring to retire. He was sixty-four. However, no

doubt to the chagrin of Stotherd, he did not leave Jaipur but stayed on as a consultant to the *darbar*.[71] He lingered on the stage for quite a while. In 1913 he was appointed by the Government of India as a special advisor to Edwin Lutyens in connection with the design of New Delhi. His role was to educate Lutyens in the use of Indian styles, deemed appropriate by the Viceroy, amongst others. Lutyens not surprisingly found his contribution peculiarly irksome, but as Jacob was by now in his seventies and anxious finally to retire completely, Lutyens was able to kick over the traces with little difficulty.[72] Jacob died in 1917.

Jacob's continued presence in the period after 1905 meant that he was on hand to supervise ongoing projects such as the Lallgarh in Bikaner, and he even undertook some new ones, in British India. He advised the architect Sydney Crookshank on the designs for Lucknow University and the King George and Queen Mary Hospital and Medical College, Lucknow (1912).[73] He also undertook the design of St John's College in Agra, in 1913,[74] a full-blooded exercise in the Indo-Saracenic mode since he was by then working alone, without the support of the Jaipur office.

When he had first left it on secondment in 1902, his deputy, Stotherd, tried valiantly to maintain the architectural workload, though his description of the department's functions in an early report implies that he had less enthusiasm for it and he considered the business of roads and irrigation more important; and indeed within a few years the design projects were greatly reduced in both size and number.[75] By then, however, a new force had emerged as a contributor to the architecture of Jaipur. As the PWD took its exit, its role had already been taken up by another department of state, the Raj Imarat, which was primarily responsible for the construction and maintenance of works for the Maharaja. Its *darogha* (director) since 1886 had been Chiman Lal, who had earlier trained in Jacob's office.[76]

A substantial addition to the palace complex, designed by this department under Chiman Lal, was made in 1900.[77] The Mubarak Mahal stands on a low podium placed centrally within a spacious courtyard immediately to the south of the main palace buildings; it is linked to the court of the Diwan-i-Khas by a gate, now called the Rajendra Pol, which was designed and made as part of a united scheme (illus. 43, 96, 125). The original function of the Mubarak Mahal is not recorded, but it is thought to have been meant as a reception hall for any visitors who were not to be admitted within the main areas of the palace. This idea is supported

by the original name of the gate, Sarhad ki Deori or 'boundary door', implying that the court of the Mubarak Mahal was originally considered as lying outside the palace proper. The gate's glittering brass doors (constructed at a cost of Rs 12,000) thus concealed the royal domain.[78] By the 1930s the Mubarak Mahal housed the offices of the Mahakma Khas, the Council of State;[79] and today it contains part of the palace museum.

Like the audience hall in the next court, with which it is aligned, the Mubarak Mahal follows the traditional building type known as *sarvato bhadra* in having a square plan and being open in the centre of each side (illus. 97). The centrality of the main openings in this case is stressed by the projecting verandas and balconies. The conventional mandalic basis of planning is here applied with geometric precision, as on each of the two storeys the square plan is subdivided into nine areas of equal size, grouped in a 3 x 3 grid. Although the entire building is covered at roof level, the central square has been conceived as an internal courtyard: there is no floor in this part between the two storeys, so that the central area rises through the core of the building as a double-height hall; and the rooms around the periphery of the upper floor look, through internal windows, over a central void – like the ranges round a *haveli* courtyard. Turning from the larger plan to the finer details, both the Mubarak Mahal and the corresponding Rajendra Pol show a level of craftsmanship that exceeds even the high standard established in the preceding years by buildings such as the Albert Hall (illus. 126).

It is tempting to conclude that the Mubarak Mahal demonstrates the *vastu vidya* system, undivided and freed from the direct intervention of a British engineer, asserting and fulfilling itself in early twentieth-century design. But it is not quite as clear as that. Although Jacob had no hand in the

96 The Mubarak Mahal, Jaipur City Palace, by the office of Chiman Lal, 1900.

building, the impact of the training he imparted to Chiman Lal and others can be seen in this design. The geometric precision of the planning, though not in itself alien to the Indian tradition, here suggests a method of design based on the drawing office rather than something worked out in the head, on site, according to guiding principles. All element of chance has been expelled on the drawing board. And those expertly executed details suggest a tradition preserved in the pages of the *Jaipur Portfolio* rather than developed through continuing practice. Gordon Sanderson writes that 'the ornament was sketched for the stone-cutters (8 annas per day) direct on the stone by draftsmen', as if to imply the continuity of a traditional practice,[80]

but his comment also reveals a very modern separation of drawing from construction, since evidently the two groups of workmen were not the same. An archaeological rather than a living spirit pervades this exquisite little building, and for all its beauty it shows that the *vastu vidya* system had been permanently changed.

Jacob's teaching is even more evident in the next major project of the Raj Imarat, the King Edward Memorial Sarai (1911–15; illus. 98), located outside the city wall on what is now Mirza Ismail Road. For this work Chiman Lal was assisted by his deputy, Bhola Nath.[81] Constructed after Jacob's removal from the centre of activity, the result is nevertheless stylistically reminiscent of some of his

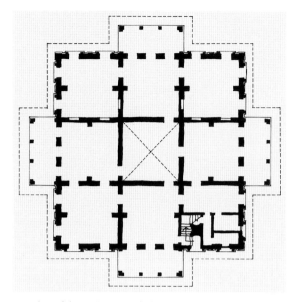

97 Plan of the Mubarak Mahal.

office's minor works. The stone-carving in particular is not an integrated element of the design but offers ornamental passages over a utilitarian structure.

The major work of the department in this period, and one that again shows Jacob's continuing legacy, was the rebuilding of the Rambagh Palace (1909–16). This building, now a famous hotel, has a complicated history. The origin was a small retreat within a garden, situated well outside the walled city, to the south-west, built early in the reign of Sawai Ram Singh, about 1835.[82] Later, Madho Singh decided to convert it into a guest house and engaged Jacob to supply the designs. This phase consists of the two wings, linked by a range of large rooms and a veranda, together forming a 'U' formation facing towards the garden on the south-

98 The King Edward Memorial Sarai, Jaipur, by Chiman Lal and Bhola Nath, 1911–15.

east, and also a great hall on the west (illus. 127, 128).[83] Jacob probably prepared these designs in the period when he was engaged by the *darbar* at the end of 1905, but they were actually carried out by the Raj Imarat under Chiman Lal and Bhola Nath between 1909 and 1916.[84] The building was completed and its new status as a palace was inaugurated by a banquet for the Viceroy, Lord Chelmsford, in November 1916. This was to be Chiman Lal's last major project, as ill-health forced him to retire in 1919.

At this stage the orientation of the building was still towards the west.[85] A third phase of construction, carried out in the mid-1930s for the last Maharaja, Sawai Man Singh II (*r.* 1922–49), entailed the attachment of three vast new wings, together framing a new courtyard on the western side, and the provision of a new entrance in the south-west corner.[86] Through all these phases the vocabulary of architectural forms – the style of arches, columns, windows and balconies and so on – remains consistently Indian, and characteristically Rajput. But their organization tells a different story. In those parts designed and built by Jacob and Chiman Lal, though the scale is European, there are some typically Indian divisions of space, with changes in floor level and screened balconies separating some parts of rooms from others. But by the time of Man Singh's additions even these traces of Indian organizing logic have disappeared.

The new ranges transformed Rambagh into a residential palace comparable to Lallgarh in Bikaner, and indeed after his marriage to his third wife in 1940, Man Singh made this his new home, where he could lead the fashionable Western lifestyle that he preferred.[87] Meanwhile, there were further developments in city planning. The Albert Hall and its surrounding formal gardens, the Ram Niwas Bagh, had represented the first phase in the development of a new town, open and spacious, to the south of the walled city; and in the 1940s this area was substantially developed, notably by the construction of Mirza Ismail Road, named after one of the last prime ministers of the independent state. Thus the closing years of royal rule in Jaipur were played out well outside the founder's walls, and beyond the bounds of the Maharaja's mandalic courts.

99 Vidhan Sabha, Jaipur.

5   Delivering the Past

When British India gained independence in 1947, the Crown's treaties with the Indian states became unworkable, as the guarantees of their sovereignty could no longer be sustained, and the diplomatic efforts particularly of India's new leaders ensured the integration of these states into the new Indian union. The major Rajput states thus amalgamated to form the new state of Rajasthan in 1949. Jaipur was selected as the capital, and so at the stroke of a pen the city became the administrative centre of a region not of 16,000 but of 340,000 square miles. The new role has placed a considerable strain on the city's infrastructure, and in the last half-century Jaipur has experienced unprecedented expansion and the growth of its population to a figure now in excess of one and a half million.

In recent years, contributions to the city have been made by two of India's most prominent architects, both of whom have declared a special interest in traditional values. In the 1980s, B. V. Doshi was commissioned to plan a vast new township named Vidyadhar Nagar, situated to the north-west of the walled city, whose original plan served as his ostensible inspiration. And that same plan also inspired Charles Correa, working on a smaller scale, in his design for the Jawahar Kala Kendra, a prestigious arts centre located to the south of old Jaipur. Respectively on a macro and a micro scale, these two projects exemplify some of

the understandings and uses of the past in the Post-Modern context. Before considering these projects in detail, however, we will examine how the building regulations and planning by-laws in force in post-Independence Jaipur attempt to preserve the city's past while providing for its present and future, and the relation of those regulations and by-laws to other planning systems, including the colonial model and *vastu vidya*.

Building By-laws

The old city of Jaipur has outlived the architectural principles on which it was built. It is now in the care of regulating authorities such as the Municipal Corporation and the Jaipur Development Authority, which together act as the guardian of its old charm, protecting it from the impingement of the new. The mere fact that the old needs protection from the new reveals the gulf that separates their architectural ideologies. There is a growing concern in India for the preservation of pre-modern structures, often achieved by isolating them from use and insulating them from contemporary design interventions. Pickled buildings in a preserve of trapped time are labelled 'lifestyle' museums, but the life they were meant to support and nurture has been extracted. The restoration of Bagore ki Haveli (built in 1671) in Udaipur is one such example, where:

Having restored the architectural heritage to its full glory, the challenge now lay in projecting the lifestyle as authentically as possible. This meant assigning each of the restored spaces an activity that was consistent with its past. In close consultation with experts and, more importantly, those familiar and with personal experience of the lifestyle that was to be recreated, artefacts and daily objects of use were purchased in original ... to ensure the authenticity of what was to become eventually India's first museum dedicated to a lifestyle.[1]

This is in line with a global trend in conservation, the conversion of old palaces into places of interest where the occasional visitor can marvel at the rich heritage of a bygone era, but this trend may not be the best solution for the Indian context. Many of the kinds of objects that are placed in such museums are still produced and used, and there seems little virtue in eliminating their 'life' from their 'style'. Old Jaipur is still a thriving, living city, offering more than the benefits of tourism. Although now bursting at its seams with the pressures of population and growth, it is still a major commercial centre, as it was some 200 years ago.

Today the eighteenth-century walled city is just one of the six sectors that constitute the region of Jaipur. Although the divisions are described by the Jaipur Development Authority as based on geographical boundaries, they separate rural from urban areas, and the old from the new. For example, Sector S–1 includes all the villages that fall within the region of Jaipur and are controlled by the village Panchayats; Sector S–2 is all urban areas controlled by the Municipal Corporation; and Sector S–3 is the part of Jaipur that falls within the old walls, the original Jaipur.[2] The building by-laws regulate building activity in each area of the city on the basis of these divisions. The Jaipur Development Authority has direct control over the infrastructural facilities provided in these areas, and influences their future development. Although it would be wrong to regard the by-laws as a modern-day *vastu shastra*, they obviously do influence building design; and they promote a certain development distinctly different from the architectural principles on which Jaipur was originally built. Indeed, if old Jaipur had to apply for planning permission from an authority that followed today's by-laws, it would fail miserably, and would be condemned for flouting all regulations. Partly, of course, this is because services such as drainage, electricity and communication systems have improved, due to technological advances that are naturally reflected in the by-laws. But more importantly, modern building design regulation throughout India has its roots firmly planted in the soil of the British PWD, and, insofar as it looks forward it aspires to echo global trends, to include 'amusement parks and Disneyland'[3] within its range of building types.

Altogether five building types are recognized, with appropriate regulations for each: residential, commercial or professional, institutional, industrial, and a 'special' type that includes cinemas, bus and railway stations, parks and other public spaces. The residential category is subdivided into farmhouses, independent plotted units, small residential schemes and multi-storey residential schemes. For each of these sub-categories there are minimum distances by which the building must be set back from its boundary wall on all sides. For example, for a 500 m² plot the regulations demand leaving clear at least 7.5 m in front, 3 m and 2.5 m on the sides, and 3 m at the back. The maximum covered area is 45 per cent of the plot and the maximum height is 12 m.[4] The height of the building must not be more than the width of the road in front. This kind of massing rules out any possibility of shaded streets and compact structures, and actively encourages a 'bungalow' type of development with houses surrounded by open spaces (illus. 100 and 101). Most builders obviously aim towards maximum coverage, and the open space around the house is considered a waste. This outdoor space has to be protected by the owners from outside encroachment, and by the regulating body from encroachment by the owner. Traditionally, the measurement of the site was the measurement of the house,

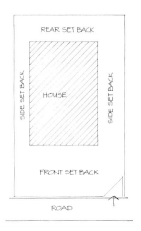 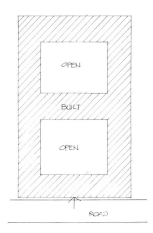

100 House with set-back (left) contrasted with the building scheme of a *haveli*.

101 New housing scheme, Jaipur Sector C.

131

and the open space was inside in the form of a court-yard, rather than outside the house. As we saw in Chapter Three, the size of the courtyard was linked to the ranges built around it. Today it is percentages that link the open and covered spaces. It makes no difference where and how the 45 per cent of the area is covered. The building regulations speak in terms of upper and lower limits, and the builders aim to maximize the maximum, and minimize the minimum, creating an environment that demands constant policing, more regulations, lengthier forms and discontent on both sides. Rather than working alongside each other, the perceived relationship between the planning authority and the designer or builder is like that of a tyrant ruler and a dissident subject, a game of cat and mouse.

At the micro scale, the constituent parts of a residential building of an area more than 50 m^2 are also prescribed in terms of minimum areas, minimum dimensions of one side and minimum heights. For example, a habitable room should be of a minimum area of 9.5 m^2, with one of its sides measuring at least 2.4 m and with a height of at least 2.75 m; a 'toilet' should be a minimum of 2.8 m^2 in area and 2.2 m in height, with one of its sides measuring at least 1.2 m.[5] Of course, the aim of the regulations is to ensure the bare minimum required for a usable space. The figures are by no means arbitrary: they are based on an anthropometric study of a British man, set out in the widely used building standards manuals. As long as the architect's plans satisfy these minimum dimensions,

102 Ganpati Plaza: a new shopping complex on land designated for commercial use.

his design is safe from being rejected. But since the enforcement is of minimum dimensions and not of optimum sizes, the minimums become norms.

At the larger scale of a small town development, the entire area is subdivided into percentages, where a maximum of 50 per cent of the land is allocated to residences; a maximum of 5 per cent to a 'convenient shop'; a minimum of 25 per cent to roads; a minimum of 15 per cent to parks, playgrounds, a 'sports complex' and community centres; and a minimum of 5 per cent to public services such as a police station, electricity and water boards, a cemetery and a hospital (illus. 102).[6] The rules therefore encourage more roads, parks and sports facilities, police stations and cemeteries, and discourage the building of houses and shops, even in a residential scheme – in stark contrast to the old city, which is packed precisely with houses and shops. The regulations presuppose a general tendency of people to build too many shops and houses, and to ignore shared areas such as public parks and roads. But even if this assumption is correct, then why should we not accept it rather than attempt to work against it? Jaipur provides an example of how to work with a mixed land use development that combines residential and commercial functions. Second, if it is the case that roads and parks are generally ignored because their upkeep is not in anyone's personal interest, then why not again learn from the case of Jaipur, where the roads are still named after the professions of their residents: this indirectly makes them responsible for them, because it is not in the interest of the tradesman to have a potential customer walk down a dirty, pitted road. Likewise, it should be possible to resolve issues of interests and responsibilities with solutions that require minimum policing and maximum voluntary control. To do this would naturally require an acceptance of the painful fact that most building regulations and mainstream methods need urgent and serious reassessment.

Indian 'Essences'

It is not as if no lessons have been learnt from old Jaipur, because now and then its design inspires new projects, especially in the surrounding region. Regarded by modern architects today as an epitome of a traditional city, old Jaipur is often analyzed by them in terms of its street pattern, with all the hustle and bustle of 'multivalent' spaces, its red sandstone hue, its complex arrangement imbued with 'symbolic and social meanings'. Within the Post-Modern world of critical regionalism, architects seek to express a visual or conceptual connection to the past, recent or remote – while stopping short of re-enacting old processes, to retain their place in the global fraternity. As Kurula Varkey explains:

> The task is demanding – to rediscover in the past the essence of its ethos; and then to redefine it and reinterpret it in a new light; in a creative renewal, for each period must reinvent its own language . . . The value systems of a culture manifest themselves in its built form – defining cultural ethos through its idiomatic expressions. In each period it takes specific expressions that constitute its period style. In [the] search for underlying principles, what is important is to distinguish the basic content from the variety of expressions and the period languages.[7]

Varkey goes on to explain that Indic architecture can be understood in terms of its 'sense of centre and statement of limits', its 'attitude to spatial organization', 'attitude to order', 'attitude to proportion', 'attitude to light', 'attitude to form' and 'attitude to symbols and meanings'.[8] Although an understanding of these concepts may help to produce a new architecture that is Indian, if not in style then at least in attitude, such bottled essences cannot produce new and different fruits and flowers. This exercise of distilling an essence that can then be infused into any form is based on the mistaken notion that the essence is produced independently of form. Nevertheless this is indeed how modern Indian architecture aspires for international acclaim, hoping that essence without form will generate a recognizable but not too Indian look. But for whose benefit? If finding an Indian essence is the solution, then who are its audience and users? The rejected local style will invariably be replaced by another style, from another region or even country. Post-Modern architects, at least at this level, seem to aim for the opposite of what the conservationists wish to achieve. The former eliminate the style to keep the use, while the latter preserve the style and eliminate the use.

Particularly revealing in this context are two architectural projects by established and highly accomplished contemporary architects. Both are prolific designers and innovators who also write and have been extensively written about, in India and abroad.[9] The first project is at the macro scale of an urban plan, while the other is at the micro scale of a single, multi-functional building. In both cases the site is just outside the walled city of Jaipur.

The cover of the March 1997 issue of the arts magazine *Marg* carried B.V. Doshi's 'concept sheet' with the proposal for a satellite town for Jaipur, called Vidyadhar Nagar, after the supposed architect of old Jaipur (illus. 103). The 'concept' silkscreen of New Jaipur (1986), is an attractive artwork in bright colours, with symbols of the sun and the moon, *purushas* and *mandalas*, Shiva *linga* and gateways; with it are Le Corbusier-style rough sketches of the site and a layout of 'fingers of greenery'[10] meandering within a geometric pattern of roads, and a slogan: 'Vidyadhar Nagar A City Symbolic of Permanence and Order Faith Safety Security and Social Economic Technical Opportunities'.[11] While the slogan may apply to any city proposal, anywhere, the rest of the imagery of the poster clearly sums up the two main influences on Doshi's design, as William Curtis explains: 'In effect, his plan crossbred aspects of Le Corbusier with aspects of old Jaipur – two powerful types based on different spiritual and intellectual ideals.'[12]

The influence of Le Corbusier was only natural. Le Corbusier had been Doshi's master, someone he admired and had worked with; he participated alongside him in a significant moment of India's modern architectural history – the building of Chandigarh in the 1950s. Doshi was less familiar, however, with the city of old Jaipur. Because of his firm belief that 'the built form must be rooted in the land where it stands',[13]

Doshi's office set up a study group to analyse old Jaipur and to distil its essential principles. This work established typical layouts, lighting angles, social uses, dimensions, façade proportions and so on.[14]

As a result he evolved his own 'pattern language' based on his findings in Jaipur and Le Corbusier's teachings, so that

The broad central avenue and the necklaces of greenery recall Chandigarh, while the tight street patterns and protective approach roads reflect ancient Indo–Aryan practice as gleaned from a reading of the scriptures.[15]

103 The concept sheet for Vidyadhar Nagar; from *Marg*, March 1997.

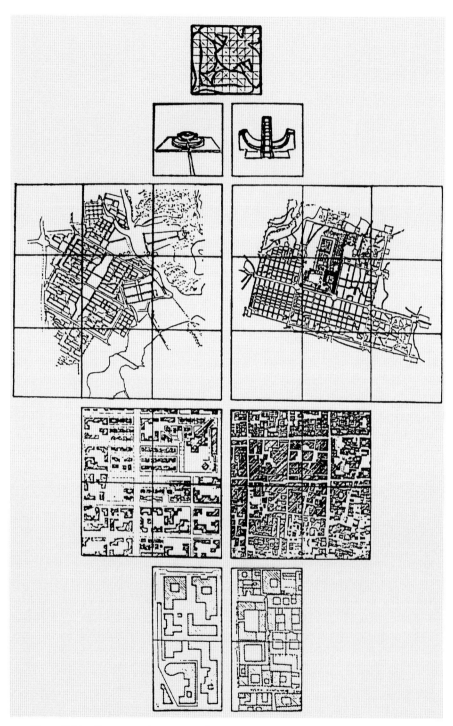

104 Plan of Vidyadhar Nagar, by B. V. Doshi.

It is too early to say whether this new neighbour of Jaipur is a success or a failure, as it is still being built (illus. 104 and 129). What is of interest here is to understand the nature of the responses that contemporary design, in its enthusiastic bid for rootedness, makes to its location of Jaipur. In the above description of the design methodology and the presentation of the Vidyadhar Nagar project, one obvious question emerges: who is it all aimed at? The simple answer is: writers and other architects. If the exchange were limited to this small coterie, it would not matter much, but its significance lies in the fact that writing on architecture and design does have a strong influence on future design and to a large extent on the reading and use of past architecture. For the benefit of this project old Jaipur was put to a laboratory test where its solar angles were measured, its massing and volumes were analyzed, its streets and squares were scrutinized, using not the tools of design that generated the city, but a completely different set of parameters, of 'essential principles'. The design proposal may have done ample justice to the legacy of Le Corbusier, but in terms of responding to its historical and geographical context it starts from a completely false premise. The modern study of old Jaipur is at two removes from the logic that shaped the city: first, it ignores the city's theoretical basis and its own principles of design; and second, it chooses a different set of tools of measurement and analysis, and then superimposes on the city a theory inferred from the results of the survey. The result is that it is now possible to read Jaipur and other 'traditional' Indian cities in terms of tight-knit patterns and textural qualities, and then incorporate those patterns in new designs propped up with 'Indian' explanations and presentations of cosmic orders and *mandalas*, and artworks.

The nine-square *mandala* has become a buzzword, a password amongst regionalists applied with equal superficiality to design statements and to the reading of old cities. But while its pattern may look convincingly 'Indian', as do the Rajasthani-styled elevations of the design, this is of little consequence to the most important player in the game of architecture, the user.

Doshi, recently commenting in general on design and workmanship said,

> There is no such thing as a bad building. It is poor design that's the problem, but it has nothing to do with detail. You design poorly, when you think poorly. We have to elevate the tastes of everybody by talking about excellence. We should also talk about institutionalization of architecture. Today architecture is not institutionalized in the country. It is not respected. It is only a tool but I think, when this tool will become an object of art, its meaning would change because it would become sacred. Until this sanctity is restored, we are not going to get meaning in a building or in detailing.[16]

Perhaps to an architect, architecture is an object of art, a permanent display of his talent, and how that object of art is perceived by the viewer may, to some degree, be shaped by the two-dimensional images and text that are included in the design package. In an ideal world, where the architect enjoys supreme control over his design and its execution, the concept design and the built form should be about roughly the same thing. The reality, however, is that the original design has been changed to a large extent, so that even the colour wash has become the 'Barbie' pink that now adorns the façades. This may be the fault of the executing contractors or the regulating bureaucracy, as

> Unfortunately, developers are becoming more powerful than the architects and I don't think the developers or the government agencies which have the capacity to change the laws, have understood what urban design is or for that matter, what cities are about. I think our bureaucracy has not understood the architectural process the way our forefathers did; that architecture or city planning or a built form, is meant to nourish life.[17]

And that is the fundamental difference between an art object and a building: architecture is about 'nourishing life', about buildings in which people lead their lives, whereas an art object bears no such responsibility. One may choose not to look at an art object, but one cannot make the same choice about shelter. Plans and elevations are a means to executing design. Abstract artworks and attractive drawings may help to sell the design to clients, but they become less important once the structure is built. The real test of the building lies with its users and how they perceive it. How will the references that the design statement of Vidyadhar Nagar makes to Old Jaipur be read by its users, if, as K. T. Ravindran puts it, there is 'a direct schism … between society at large and us, the trained architects'?

> The subtle, abstract forms that we worship often leave the average city dweller in India cold . . . The clue, I think, lies in the fact that sources of abstraction as much as their vehicles are sourced within the meaning-pool of the social milieu. The contradiction between communicability and abstraction is something

that every contemporary architect in India faces some time or the other. Some of us have bluffed our way through it, others have made commercial disasters of themselves and some have given up in the middle. Few have confronted and come to terms with this great dilemma of contemporary architecture in India.[18]

Old Jaipur has another important lesson to teach in this regard. The site was laid out, and the basic framework of streets, squares and plots established. Businessmen and professionals were then invited to build on those plots. No two houses or buildings are the same in the old city, and yet it exudes a homogeneous character. The success of such an operation lies in a perfect communication between the vision and reality. All three components of the 'bureaucracy' – the patron and his officers; the designers, builders and craftsmen; and the users – were in tune with each other. Ideas were sold and bought, designs weak and strong were built, but all within one shared architectural system and ideology. The criterion for grouping is professional, so that inhabitants can share and look after the common facilities they require for the production and sale of their produce. Potters share kilns, dyers share drying space, shoemakers can share tanneries. The modern-day housing schemes are grouped around economic criteria, which say little about the users, apart from their buying power. With Vidyadhar Nagar, as with most new government housing development schemes, the user is a largely absent force, making little or no input in its design. Vidyadhar Nagar incorporates a mixed land use, mixing shops and houses (an influence of the old Jaipur scheme), but no one seems to have asked who will be the shopkeepers, where will they live, and what will they sell and produce: a consideration that was closely monitored in the case of the old city.

In 1959, the young Charles Correa, participating in the first ever seminar on architecture in post-Independence India, said:

Sometimes I think it is very lucky for us that we are living in India. It permits us to feel very virtuous, defending our work in the name of Gropius, Corbusier, etc. If we were to build these same buildings in the middle of – say – New York or Milan or Tokyo, I wonder who would defend them.[19]

He was ahead of his time, as it was already clear to him, amid the euphoria of new technologies and nationalistic fervour, that modern buildings in India had to justify themselves outside India, as being Indian. One way in which this could be achieved is by using Indian words to decorate the brief, because:

The prosaic architecture we create today is not due just to the banality of the forms we construct but also to the mundane briefs we address (which, in turn, I guess, reflect the kind of lives we all lead) . . . The sacred realm is a crucial part of our environment, but over the last few decades we have increasingly blanked it out of our conciousness.[20]

A brief made interesting by incorporating 'myth', along with aspects of Indian concepts and symbols that are 'transformed' beyond recognition of pastiche, briefly sums up Correa's recipe for overcoming the 'Indian' problem. He explains the necessity of 'transformation':

Architecture based on the superficial *transfer* of images from another culture or another age cannot survive; architecture must be generated from the *transformation* of those images, that is, by expressing anew the mythic beliefs that underlie the images.[21]

His example of *transfer* (by which he seems to mean 'lesser architecture') is 'European architecture in India', and examples of *transformations* (apparently 'greater architecture') are the Diwan-i-Khas in Fatehpur Sikri, Jaipur, Le Corbusier's Chandigarh (called 'true transformation'), the work of Alvar Aalto in Finland and of Frank Lloyd Wright. What follows is his explanation of Jaipur as an example of transformation. The reason for quoting Correa's ideas about Jaipur is not to show that they are ill informed. The point is to illustrate how a reading (or misreading) of past architecture can directly influence future design.

The second example of transformation is the plan for the city of Jaipur, built in the eighteenth century in Rajasthan. Jaipur represents a transformation of another kind [the first example being Fatehpur Sikri, which is 'a transformation of staggering metaphysical and political impact']. Maharaja Jai Singh, who founded the city, was also the renowned astronomer who built the five *jantar mantars* (observatories) at Delhi, Jaipur, Ujjain, Banaras, and Allahabad. In the planning of Jaipur he embarked on a truly extraordinary venture. He sought to combine his passion for the latest tenets of contemporary astronomy with the most ancient and sacred of his beliefs. The plan of the city is based on a nine-square *mandala* corresponding to the *navagraha* or nine planets. The void in the central square he used for the palace garden. (Because of the presence of a hill, a corner square was moved diagonally across.)

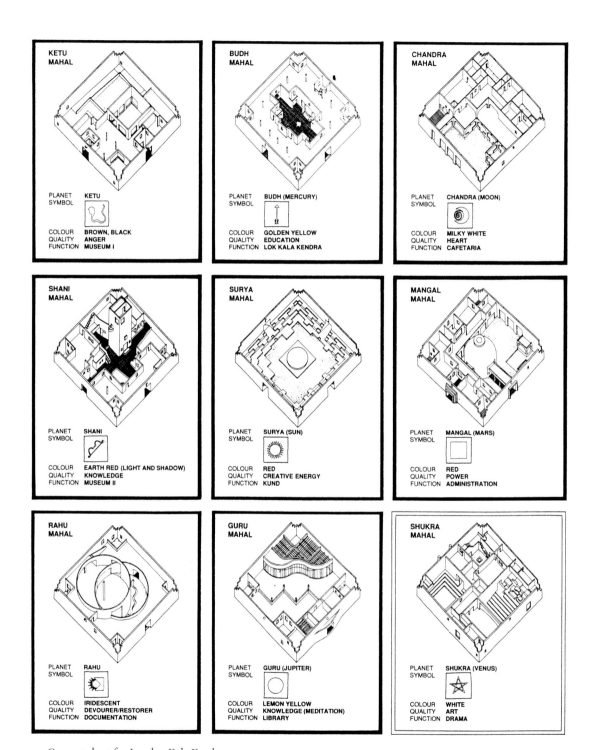

KETU MAHAL

PLANET SYMBOL	KETU
COLOUR	BROWN, BLACK
QUALITY	ANGER
FUNCTION	MUSEUM I

BUDH MAHAL

PLANET SYMBOL	BUDH (MERCURY)
COLOUR	GOLDEN YELLOW
QUALITY	EDUCATION
FUNCTION	LOK KALA KENDRA

CHANDRA MAHAL

PLANET SYMBOL	CHANDRA (MOON)
COLOUR	MILKY WHITE
QUALITY	HEART
FUNCTION	CAFETARIA

SHANI MAHAL

PLANET SYMBOL	SHANI
COLOUR	EARTH RED (LIGHT AND SHADOW)
QUALITY	KNOWLEDGE
FUNCTION	MUSEUM II

SURYA MAHAL

PLANET SYMBOL	SURYA (SUN)
COLOUR	RED
QUALITY	CREATIVE ENERGY
FUNCTION	KUND

MANGAL MAHAL

PLANET SYMBOL	MANGAL (MARS)
COLOUR	RED
QUALITY	POWER
FUNCTION	ADMINISTRATION

RAHU MAHAL

PLANET SYMBOL	RAHU
COLOUR	IRIDESCENT
QUALITY	DEVOURER/RESTORER
FUNCTION	DOCUMENTATION

GURU MAHAL

PLANET SYMBOL	GURU (JUPITER)
COLOUR	LEMON YELLOW
QUALITY	KNOWLEDGE (MEDITATION)
FUNCTION	LIBRARY

SHUKRA MAHAL

PLANET SYMBOL	SHUKRA (VENUS)
COLOUR	WHITE
QUALITY	ART
FUNCTION	DRAMA

105 Concept sheet for Jawahar Kala Kendra.

Jaipur's plan is worthy of admiration: for the clarity of its main arteries, the efficiency of its water-management system, the understanding of essential socio-economic patterns, and above all, for the startling relevance to us today of the transformation between past and future, between material and metaphysical worlds, among public, private, and sacred realms that Maharaja Jai Singh sought to synthesize.[22]

Basing his design on this story of the plan of Jaipur, Correa built an arts centre just outside the old city. The design of Jawahar Kala Kendra (1986)

is a diagrammatic representation of his myth, readable only in his plan of nine squares (illus. 105 and 106). It is composed of nine squares, with one square in the north-east skewed, making way for a corner entrance to the complex. Each of the nine squares carries a planetary theme and associated symbols, colours and functions, which have been 'reinvented' for the story, to make a mundane brief interesting. The central square is an open-air theatre and exhibition space that is styled to resemble the *kund* at Modhera in Gujarat. This square is central only in terms of the geometry of the plan, and not in terms of its function. The circulation within the building does not lead one into

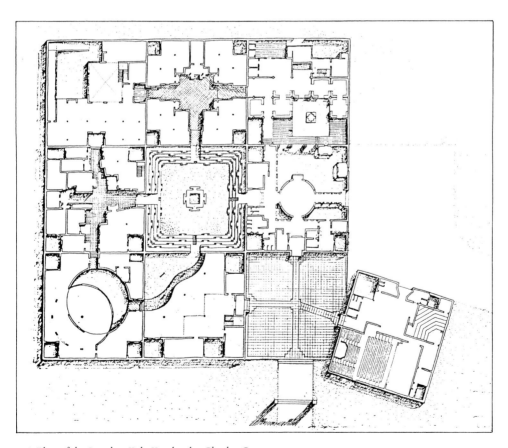

106 Plan of the Jawahar Kala Kendra, by Charles Correa.

this space, and it has no connection with the other parts of the building (illus. 107 and 130). The symbolism and myth that Correa employs in this building would escape the notice of someone who has not read the explanatory notes in the journals, and is not familiar with an aerial view of its design. In this regard, again, the design is conceived as a work of art.

In defence of this remarkable project – and indeed of Doshi's urban plan – one might ask whether it matters that the architect's design shows a scanty understanding of the historical context. Even in public projects, the modern architect claims – and is generally granted – a licence to make whatever use of the past he or she pleases, provided only that the client is persuaded. And certainly the results in these two cases have considerable aesthetic appeal. It would be pedantic (and unhistorical) to count the solecisms they commit against the shastric canon. The designs are free expressions, which engage with history on their own terms. The irony lies in how that cherished individuality subverts the intention to communicate. Both architects have sincerely and earnestly striven to infuse their designs with an Indian identity, and to achieve this they have appealed to a shared and inherited architectural language; but their imaginative reinventions of that language as private and personal vocabularies of symbols and forms redirect its communicative

107 Jawahar Kala Kendra, interior, with exhibition space.

108 Vidhan Sabha, Jaipur, by Rajasthan State PWD; completed 2001.

force. The craftsmen of Jaipur who are not trained in the ways of the urban architect but who retain some understanding of shastric norms ought naturally to form the ideal audience. But to such people the projects' Indian identity is invisible, even as it secures the desired accolades from a wider, global constituency.

That these projects are locally perceived as élitist and idiosyncratic can be measured in part by their lack of influence on subsequent public buildings. The most recent major addition to Jaipur's architectural fabric is the vast new Vidhan Sabha, an assembly building for Rajasthan's regional government legislators, designed by architects of the state Public Works Department and completed in 2001 (illus. 99, 108). In some ways this design is a return to the approach of the Indo-Saracenic movement, with indigenizing motifs deployed as a magnificent camouflage over the building's structure. The approach is taken one step further only in the complete separation of the two

layers: the splendid arcades that sweep across its façades, being three storeys high, provide no shade or circulation to the spaces within, and they function only as bearers of identity. The elephants sculpted on the entrance gates imitate those on the screen before Lutyens's palace in New Delhi; and along with the Ashokan lions over the dome, they hint at imperial pretentions nestling within this regional authority – a spirit that would not have been strange to the city's founder. But whatever it may tell us about Jaipur's present political self-assertion, the Vidhan Sabha plainly reveals that architecturally all is confusion.

109 LIC Centre, New Delhi, by Charles Correa, 1975–86.

6 The Uses of *Vastu Vidya*

This final chapter moves beyond Jaipur to develop more general arguments about the relation of *vastu vidya* to architectural practice in the past, about its current uses and about its future potential. We are thus engaging in at least two current debates. The first, conducted chiefly by art historians, concerns the role of *vastu vidya* historically and its usefulness in understanding the monuments of the past. The second is a much wider one, involving architects and also members of the general public as their patrons and consumers, and concerns the role and relevance of *vastu vidya* in architectural design and building construction today. Unfortunately, the fact that these two debates (involving as they do different personnel) have hitherto largely been conducted in isolation from each other has been an obstacle to progress in either, as our simultaneous intervention in both will demonstrate.

Past Applications: The State of Scholarship

The question of how *vastu vidya* functioned in the past – in particular the relationship between a literary genre of *vastu shastra* on the one hand and architectural traditions on the other – has not yet been satisfactorily resolved. To a considerable extent, this is a reflection of scholarly convention, as the two domains have had too little contact with

each other. Work on the texts of *vastu shastra* has tended to remain the preserve of expert linguists and literary scholars who have been concerned to render the texts accessible to others but commonly lack the knowledge base required to tie their interpretations to the built traditions. One obvious example of this is P. K. Acharya's work on *Manasara* (1934). The linguistic study of the text is exhaustive and impressive, but in spite of the author's claims to consider its relation to architectural history (especially in volume 6 of his series[1]), he offers very little in the way of analysis of extant buildings. He is generally more concerned to relate the text of *Manasara* to other texts, especially those of the Western classical tradition, such as Vitruvius, and such comparisons, unprompted as they are by any actual historical connections, obscure more than they clarify. In a similar vein, Tarapada Bhattacharya, in his seminal work on *The Canons of Indian Art* (1947), displays a wide-ranging knowledge of the texts and of their intellectual context, relating them to the *Rg Veda* and to the epics but not to specific historical buildings. Another ground-breaking textual study, by D. N. Shukla (1958–60), includes some discussion of buildings but at a very general level, ungrounded in architectural expertise.

On the other side of the scholarly divide, the analysis of architectural traditions has mostly been conducted by architectural historians for whom even the translated texts apparently remain obscure and unhelpful in such habitual projects as the definition of style, the description of morphological evolution and even the observation of function. To them the *vastu* texts are apt to seem arcane and impractical, concerned only with mysterious rites and with developing elaborate systems of classification, which may be intellectually elegant but can have little practical value. A good example of this – chosen here precisely because it manages so successfully to elucidate in close detail aspects of the structure, form and meaning of historical buildings without any reference to *vastu shastra* – is the recent work of Adam Hardy (1994), the basis of whose method is the empirical investigation of the built form itself. This is not to suggest that reference to the texts would necessarily undermine Hardy's deductions – indeed it might be expected to reinforce them – but to note that any such reference is explicitly judged to be superfluous. A more conventional example of this approach is the earlier work of Percy Brown (1942), which surveys the entire field of Indian architecture and places monuments in stylistic categories, again without any reference to the building theories that informed their design; and his procedure has retained a dominant place in the discipline for half a century.[2]

A few conspicuous attempts to bring together these two domains of scholarship have not been fully successful. Stella Kramrisch's famous and much cited study of *The Hindu Temple* (1946) has always divided opinion about its merits, but in this context it could not sincerely be pointed to as achieving the desired resolution: in often vague language, it presents almost mystical paraphrases of the texts and of related religious ideas, juxtaposed with images and descriptions of temples, with no graspable account of how each illuminates the other. Alice Boner (1982) worked on both the

shastric and the architectural traditions of Orissa, providing much new insight into both; but again readers hoping to find their relationship defined might be forgiven for feeling less than satisfied. A more rigorous attempt was made through the medium of a conference organized by Anna L. Dallapiccola in 1989; this certainly succeeded in bringing representatives of the two domains into contact and discussion but, as some of the leading contributors regretfully concluded, the event in the end served principally to demonstrate the width of the gulf.[3]

Progress is impeded because the argument has tended to focus on the question of whether the *shastra* texts are to be seen as prescriptive or as descriptive; that is to say, whether they are sets of rules establishing procedures to be followed faithfully by architects (as was believed, for example, by P. K. Acharya), or on the other hand – as is frequently asserted by those who are sceptical about the closeness of the relationship – whether they constitute a purely literary genre in which Brahmins rationalized (according to their own accustomed intellectual systems) architectural traditions that had evolved independently. A comparison of the texts with the built environment cannot settle this dispute because the empirical evidence is inconsistent: correspondences can certainly be found, but so too can apparent discrepancies. Anyone favouring the 'prescriptive' theory may seize on the correspondences as evidence of obedient fulfilment and overlook the discrepancies or dismiss them as aberrations. Contrastingly, anyone favouring the 'descriptive' theory can point to the discrepancies as evidence that the rules did not matter much to craftsmen, and rationalize the observable correspondences by admitting that the texts' authors could on occasion accurately describe what was already before their eyes.

We suggest that this conventional dispute must always be inconclusive because its very terms are wrong. To suggest that *vastu shastras* are prescriptive is to suppose that theory is logically (if not actually chronologically) anterior to building practice; that the necessary procedure is to elaborate a paradigm of architecture and then build in accordance with it. Equally and oppositely, the 'descriptive' theory accords architectural form logical priority over theory, supposing that people first build and then rationalize what they have done. Neither of these models is logically possible. An architectural theory cannot formulate a practice out of nothing (any more than one could invent a grammar without a language); articulating a theory presupposes a tradition to mould, material to order. But equally it is impossible to build anything at all without having some system by which to order one's methods (any more than one could invent a language without a grammar). One does not precede the other; each presupposes the other. They are the two indivisible aspects of a single activity or domain. It is this unified domain that we refer to as *vastu vidya*, encompassing both the textual tradition of *vastu shastra* and architectural forms. What needs to be elucidated is not so much their relationship to each other, but the relation that each has to the body of knowledge of which each is a different kind of expression, namely *vastu vidya*.

Our study of the Ramachandra Temple led to the conclusion that the application of the texts was not prescriptive; that it was not a matter of looking up the rules in a textbook and then applying them on site. Equally, we noted that the texts do not describe this or any other specific building (as opposed to type). The texts are neither manuals nor art histories. Rather, both the temple and the texts reveal the same system for ordering a building. Both show the same approach to the ordering of its parts, from the broad layout to fine detail (such as the relative proportions of the elements of an arch). Both building and texts engage in the same structuring logic, and belong to the same field of knowledge and activity.

A Definition of *Vastu Vidya*

Vastu vidya is a body of knowledge. It can be instantiated in words, as in a *vastu shastra*, with or without support from diagrams, and also in built form. It consists of a set of concepts for organizing and structuring any building. For example, the *vastu purusha mandala* and the orientation principles (often today perceived as the core elements) are models for the organization of space and form within a building, for the disposition of the building's various functions in relation to each other and to the building's fabric. These models are mental constructs rather than physical ones. So the *vastu purusha mandala* is a square grid; it is not (as is often thought) a ground plan. Employing the *mandala* does not mean that every building has to be square in plan – evidently so, since there exist many buildings within the Indian traditions that are not. Rather, the point is that any plan, whatever its shape, can be conceived in terms of the *mandala*, in the sense that it contains a central space and peripheral zones, has direction and accommodates a range of functions. The fashionable practice of taking a drawn *mandala* and superimposing it over a drawn ground plan to test the exactness of the fit therefore mistakes the nature of its use: the pattern of a plan can be structured by a *mandala* without slavishly mirroring it. The *mandala* is not a ground plan off-the-peg but a system for achieving coherence in a plan such as can readily be understood by a user of the building who is familiar with the system.

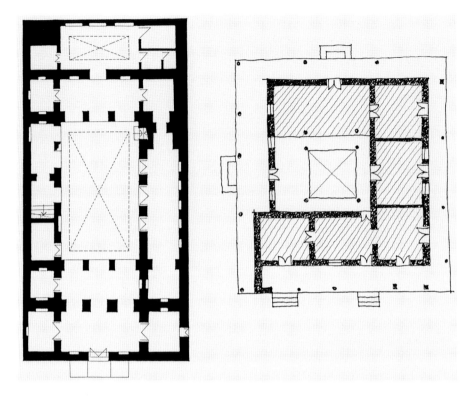

110 Differing configurations of the *mandala* as house: a Rajasthani *haveli* (left) and a Keralan *nayar tharavad* (right).

Nor are the *mandala* and the orientation principles the only content of *vastu vidya*. It also contains ideas on the organization of the whole site, to accommodate its directional and topographical specificities. It includes models of basic building types – and again, these are not prescriptive patterns but classifications of the various possibilities, such as a house of so many ranges or courtyards, or of so many storeys, and so on. It offers that most elementary tool of the building trade, a system of measurement. It contains ideas about the appropriate selection and use of conventional materials, and it defines the division of responsibility between the various members of the architectural team. All of these elements are not a random collection of ideas; their interrelation establishes them as a coherent and complete system for building design.

Thus defined, *vastu vidya* should be thought of as a system of knowledge that does not exist independently of its various built and written expressions. Because it is a set of concepts not of rules, these expressions can be very diverse. For example, the *vastu purusha mandala* informs the very different configurations of the typical Rajasthani *haveli* and the *nayar tharavad* house of Kerala (illus. 110).[4] Each characteristically has a concentric pattern around a central courtyard, but the disposition of the structural parts is very different, as are the materials, reflecting the widely differing regional conditions between Rajasthan and Kerala. *Vastu shastra* texts from these two regions – such as *Rajavallabh* and *Manushyalaya Chandrika* – differ from each other in precisely corresponding ways, as the regional authors found it appropriate to emphasize and develop different aspects of the common body of knowledge. These are just two examples. In the various regions of the subcontinent, and at various periods in its history, an enormous variety of architectural traditions has arisen. Leaving aside those traditions that relate to quite distinct (and often imported) theories of architecture, most of these traditions relate in much the same way to the wider body of knowledge, differing from each other because of the diversity in regional and historical conditions. Attempting to count these traditions would involve much arbitrary judgement since none is wholly distinct, and each existed in a continual state of development and change. The point is that *vastu vidya*, in different places and times, has been embodied in different but related ways, each of which participates in and contributes to the general body. There is no original, central or pure *vastu vidya* lying between them all; *vastu vidya* as a whole is the aggregate of all of its diverse expressions.

The Colonial Period

This very general application of *vastu vidya* within the Indian traditions historically contrasts sharply with its marginalized and fragmentary use in Indian architecture today. To explain how this remarkable change came about a brief review of some of the historical phases described in this book is necessary. Amongst the unrelated architectural traditions depending on imported paradigms, mentioned above, are some of those introduced as a consequence of British colonialism between the late eighteenth century and the mid-twentieth. The Western classical and Gothic forms of building that are typical especially of the first half of this period, although they allowed some modification in response to local materials and climate, adhered closely to European concepts and even specific

models, and so introduced into public architecture in India procedures that owe nothing to *vastu vidya*. These Western styles and their related procedures were swiftly adopted by many Indian patrons and designers, even in some of the Indian or 'Princely' states (though not much, as it happens, in Jaipur).

The disjunction between colonial and indigenous architecture was widely recognized, and in the latter part of the colonial period (after 1870) some attempt was made to narrow the divide. Encouraged by the political support of governors, viceroys and maharajas, some architects of the British Raj (and later their Indian associates) developed a new form of architecture, intended to declare the Indian identity and location of British and princely rule, giving rise to the Indo-Saracenic movement (see Chapter Four). It was not, however, to the logic or theory of Indian architecture – to *vastu vidya* – that these architects turned in their quest to indigenize their designs, but to aspects of historical imagery or style; they drew inspiration from the forms and details of a wide variety of historical monuments in the subcontinent, though with a definite emphasis on those that had been produced by the Islamic regimes that preceded British rule.

The leading practitioners of the Indo-Saracenic movement, such as Chisholm, Mant, Emerson, Wittet and Esch, designed numerous arresting pastiches in which different historical styles were imitated or combined, with varying degrees of fidelity, and grafted onto modern buildings, such as railway stations and museums, serving functions unknown in the period when the chosen styles had been developed. Eccentric as their project may seem today, its method had much in common with the historicist approach to architecture prevailing in Victorian and Edwardian Britain (Emerson, for example, had been trained by the great neo-

Gothicist William Burges). For knowledge of their local sources, the Indo-Saracenicists depended to a large extent on British scholarship, consulting the recent research on India's architectural history by authorities such as Alexander Cunningham and James Fergusson. Their approach to the reuse of Indian architectural design, however, was not so much textbook as scrapbook. Selected motifs from the past – a dome, a *chhatri*, a *jharokha*, an arch, a moulding – were torn from their original contexts and pasted onto a modern building like a form of camouflage. The underlying order of the buildings, the ideas that governed their structure and layout, remained Western, and no attempt was made to assimilate or follow Indian design methods or concepts. The Indo-Saracenic architects were vociferous in their insistence that architecture in India should remain Indian, and their efforts secured at least the survival in British India of the *appearance* of Indian design; but the price paid was the severance of the appearance from the logic, the vocabulary from the grammar. Indian-ness came to be expressible through motifs rather than through the *vidya* which had previously ordered them.

A second, related, consequence of colonial policy was that the integrated indigenous system of designing and building became increasingly fragmented and marginalized. The Indo-Saracenic architects claimed to be wholly dependent on Indian craftsmen for the execution of their designs, and indeed they were; but they were dependent on the craftsmen's technical skills not their design methodology – two elements that had not previously been considered as separate. Indian craftsmen made a vital contribution to the Indo-Saracenic movement, which was duly acknowledged; but this process entailed a colonial redefinition of their methods and functions. Those Indian master builders or *mistris* who continued to

practise an integrated system were mostly excluded from public and civic architecture, where their expertise was not required; thus they lost much of their customary patronage, and were restricted to the fields of sacred and domestic architecture. Here their accustomed methods continued to have some application, ensuring for the time the survival of their skills and knowledge: a report commissioned by the Archaeological Survey of India in 1913 concluded that the traditions of the *mistri* were still vigorous, though they were greatly reduced in scope.[5]

The divide between colonial and Indian architectural methodologies, and the consequences for the Indian system, did not pass wholly unnoticed at the time, and some attempts were made to redress a situation that many deplored. The work of people such as Swinton Jacob in Jaipur, Lockwood Kipling in Lahore and F. S. Growse in Bulandshahr centred on a recognition of the desirability of handing back to the craftsmen more of their functions. Collectively such attempts might be seen as constituting an Indian revival; but productive though they were, they were not greatly successful in influencing government policy or public taste and in retrospect their significance seems more symbolic than practical. They deserve attention because they indicate an alternative approach to the architectural definition of Indian identity in a modern age.

The work of such people and the evidence of the Archaeological Survey of India report led some – notably E. B. Havell – to urge the employment of *mistris* and the Indian guild system for the construction of the buildings of New Delhi (1912–31). In spite of some enthusiasm amongst those interested in the arts, this proposal never gained much political support, and the work was entrusted to British architects, with Indian craftsmen engaged, as

111 Part of South Block, New Delhi, by Herbert Baker, 1912–31.

usual, only in executing the designs (illus. 113). By this time, in any event, the traditional Indian architect–builder had begun to be eclipsed not only by foreigners but also by a new breed of Indian architect. From the late nineteenth century, architecture programmes had begun to be introduced in the schools of art, notably the J.J. School in Bombay; and though they took some account of Indian architectural ornament, the core of these curricula was based on Western methods. For the execution of their designs, the architects of the PWD had long relied not only on craftsmen but also on Indian engineers, trained in government colleges (notably that at Roorkee). The introduction of architectural programmes in the art schools ensured that by the time of Independence these engineers had been joined by a generation of Indian architects, trained in Western methods, poised to assume control of public building when the colonial regime departed.[6]

Enter the International Modern Movement

Independent India thus inherited the structures and procedures of the colonial state, the only immediate change being one of personnel.[7] Many of the most conspicuous projects of the central and regional Public Works Departments in the immediate post-Independence period – buildings such as the Ashoka Hotel and the Supreme Court in New Delhi, and the Vidhana Soudha in Bangalore – anticipate Jaipur's new Vidhan Sabha by adopting an approach directly analogous to that of the Indo-Saracenic movement, with Indian motifs scattered over the surface of a modern building (illus. 112).

A period of a very few years separates Independence in 1947 from an event that was seen at the time, and has justly continued to be seen

since, as a major turning point in Indian architecture: the appointment of Le Corbusier to design the new capital of Punjab at Chandigarh (illus. 113). The appointment of a celebrated leader of the International Modern Movement was in tune with the post-colonial, Nehruvian vision of India as a progressive participant in international developments. Much has been written about Le Corbusier's work in India, and there is no need for further detailed analysis here.[8] Of course the example of Le Corbusier was not unique: his appointment was paralleled by that of Louis Kahn to produce the designs for Dhaka in what is now Bangladesh; and both men were attracted by Gujarati patrons to work in Ahmadabad. Arguably, some of the techniques and methods of Modernism had reached India before the transfer of power. But through their politically significant and visually arresting projects, Le Corbusier and Louis Kahn introduced a whole generation of Indian architects and their clients to a new paradigm of architecture, showing them what the International Modern Movement was and how it could be grafted in their own soil. The extent to which the architects' response was merely visual rather than programmatic is a matter for argument;[9] what is beyond dispute is that they rapidly learnt a new way of building, new forms, materials and techniques, and a new rationale, logic and rhetoric. In some cases the didactic process was very direct – B. V. Doshi, for example, worked in Le Corbusier's team at Ahmadabad – but even for those less closely involved the example of the master was potent. This is everywhere evident in Indian design of the later 1950s and the 1960s, as for example in the work of Shiv Nath Prasad and the early work of both B. V. Doshi and Charles Correa (illus. 114 and 115). They and others were at first anxious to jettison any images of tradition, anything that

112 The Supreme Court, New Delhi, by the Delhi PWD, 1955.

113 The Palace of Assembly, Chandigarh, by Le Corbusier, 1951–58.

114 Tagore Hall, Ahmadabad, by B. V. Doshi, 1960s.

115 Sri Ram Arts Centre, New Delhi, by Shiv Nath Prasad, 1960s.

154

smacked of the past, in their eagerness to embrace Modernism and Internationalism.

A by-product of this new mood that is relevant here was the further widening of the gulf between the still newly established architectural profession and the surviving legacy of *vastu vidya*. The latter was now placed firmly outside the mainstream profession and became the preserve of unemployed practitioners and of a decreasing band of skilled craftsmen who mostly found themselves excluded from the building site even more rigorously than they had been during the colonial period. No longer required even for carving the ornament of Indo-Saracenic buildings, the traditional architects and craftsmen lost ground too in domestic design with the burgeoning fashion for modern-style housing.

If the Nehruvian vision of Modernism and progress tended to leave *vastu vidya* stranded, the principal alternative political vision of post-Independence India, the Gandhian one, was no more helpful because its idea of tradition was so firmly tied to the rural domain. By this view architectural 'tradition' could be respected, even admired, only so long as it was identified with the mostly mud and thatch architecture of the villages. And so this opened up another gulf: this time between traditional rural and traditional urban modes of building. Within *vastu vidya* the two are not discrete domains but are subject to the same approach and mentality; for any building project the location and the material are certainly important but they are not governing or defining features so much as elements which, along with others, are negotiated within a common set of ordering principles. The identification of 'traditional' with rural forms, and the consequent occlusion of urban tradition, was illogical. It proceeded from Modernism's displacement of urban tradition and the failure of Modern Indian architecture in its early

stages to offer much to rural India. The 1960s thus saw if anything a strengthening of a set of associations that were characteristic of the colonial period, namely 'urban' and 'modern' as opposed to 'rural' and 'traditional'.

Most professional architects in this period – and the majority still – saw, or thought they saw, very good reasons to ignore *vastu vidya*. These are discussed below, but first it is worth pausing to consider some of the standard views and prejudices as they arose in the early Modern period in India. One group of assumptions clusters around the idea that *vastu vidya* is archaic: having ancient origins and a long history, it surely cannot confront the problems of the modern age; devised for the past it cannot address the present and the future in the widest ways, most notably with regard to matters such as technology, for it has nothing of utility to say about steel, glass and concrete. A second kind of complaint is that the solutions offered by *vastu vidya* are ideals; that they presuppose unlimited space and uniform conditions. The training of modern architects prepares them to think of design in terms of site-specific solutions, to regard the peculiarities of each site as presenting challenges that then structure the design, a process in which the supposedly general prescriptions of *vastu vidya* would offer no assistance. Third, the approach of *vastu vidya* was often perceived as inflexible and rigid, leaving too little space for individual creativity and design freedom.

A full and proper understanding of the content and historical role of *vastu vidya* would reveal all of these doubts and prejudices to be misplaced. From our account of its application in Jaipur from the city's foundation up to the mid-nineteenth century, it is evident, in the first place, that *vastu vidya* may have early roots but it was never an unchanging law. For many centuries it was an evolving tradition, always adapting itself according to social change and geographical and historical diversity. It can – and has – incorporated new materials, and the potential for further development here is open. Second, though the textual solutions are indeed often general, they presuppose specific applications; in the texts and even more visibly in the built expressions, the peculiarities of each site are fully acknowledged, nowhere more clearly than in the plan of the city of Jaipur. And third, the flexibility of the design concept gives very considerable scope for creativity and diversity – again as the built expressions amply illustrate, there are an infinite number of ways of applying it. Mid-twentieth-century reservations about *vastu vidya* came not from an informed judgement about its continuing usefulness, but from the impatience of a profession that had arisen in complete ignorance of it and was fired by enthusiasm for foreign imports and novelty.

Current Applications

Recent decades have seen some alterations in this situation. Practitioners of various types have turned again to *vastu vidya* for inspiration in their activities, with the result that it has once again emerged as a topic of concern and controversy. In no case is this a return to the complete programme and methodology of *vastu vidya*; it is rather a matter of finding within *vastu vidya* some element that appears to endorse or flavour each practitioner's particular interests. The integrated system of *vastu vidya* remains as neglected and marginalized as it has been through most of the last hundred years, and its current applications continue to be partial or fragmentary. What follows is a brief survey of some of these current applications, as a prelude to a discussion of its unrealized potential.

In India, as elsewhere, a measure of dissatisfaction with the International Modern Movement was experienced within the architectural profession almost as soon as they had firmly established it. This alteration came about in part because of the dismaying realization that the pursuit of Modernism could win for Indian architects only a secondary place in terms of international recognition. The question of the domestic public response was perhaps largely irrelevant: in the initial stages the architects' excitement with the new language of Modernism was shared by a small band of influential patrons, and subsequently the wider public participated in terms of their housing aspirations, but with regard to major civic projects they accepted Modernism with incomprehension or indifference. What counted for more was the response of international cognoscenti, who, for the most part, were reluctant to applaud post-Corbusian Indian Modernism or to accord it equal status with their own, and searched instead for indications of Indian locality or identity. The project for India's leading architects then became to establish a new form of architecture. This would not entail an outright rejection of Modernism, since there could be no relinquishing of its procedures, technology or ideology, which constituted the core values of their own professional education. Rather, these elements were to be retained, while in the place of its internationalizing and universalizing tendencies some regional quality was to be re-asserted. Paradoxically the swapping of international for regional identity was sought precisely to ensure international acclaim, coinciding as it did with those preoccupations elsewhere that are loosely grouped under the umbrella term Post-Modernism.

The attempt to re-establish a regional identity within the framework of Modernism became a dominant preoccupation in the course of the 1970s; it was spearheaded by some leading architects including Charles Correa, B. V. Doshi and Raj Rewal, though it was swiftly taken up by innumerable others and discussed by critics and observers. Different methods of invoking a regional base have been attempted, sometimes involving direct references to indigenous built traditions. From the start, however, such solutions have been beset by anxieties about indulging in pastiche: there has been a fear that too literal a use of past forms would reintroduce into the design process an element of 'image-making' which the Modernist ideology had rigorously excluded. These anxieties, deeply felt, proceeded then from the architects' shared conceptual base within the Modernist paradigm, strengthened by their disdain for the products of the historicist approaches of the late colonial era.[10]

Some architects, most notably Raj Rewal, have boldly made reference in their designs to the materials, massing and motifs of historical monuments – in Rewal's case especially, the sandstone facing and *chhatris* of Mughal and Rajasthani architecture and the morphology of cities such as Jaisalmer (illus. 116 and 117). The difficulties that such an approach necessarily encounters are revealed by the architects' accompanying statements, in which they emphasize their reinterpretation of traditional forms in terms of contemporary preoccupations: they are not copying past styles but evoking traditional urban tissues, or a play of light and shade. This could be taken as a tacit recognition that there has been no reliance on traditional architectural logic or *vastu vidya* (in spite of a penchant for employing a vocabulary of *shastra* and *rasa*). Furthermore, their claims, often

supported by critics, that their use of the past is no superficial matter of imagery is somewhat belied by the habit of juxtaposing images of past and present to establish the connections.[11]

Consequently, the conundrum still facing architects, put briefly, is how to make a reference to regional sources sufficiently emphatic to be noticed without being so obvious as to open oneself to the charge of manipulating historical styles. The use of historical monuments, however it is rationalized, seems fraught with danger. Amongst the attempted resolutions to – or evasions of – this conundrum, two are especially relevant here.

One has been to note the lingering association of 'traditional' with 'rural', and so to turn to rural vernacular forms as a source of inspiration. Spurning historical monuments as self-evidently representative of the past, some have seen in the villages a continuing and living tradition, a repository of essential Indian-ness. An exploratory effort along these lines is the Gandhi Smarak Sangrahalaya in Ahmadabad, designed as early as 1958 by a youthful Charles Correa, where the limited repertoire of simple materials and the disaggregation of the various spatial elements were intended to evoke village principles (illus. 118). Correa returned to these concerns much later in his role as architect co-ordinator of the Handicrafts Museum at Pragati Maidan in New Delhi. In both these cases the references to village forms was no doubt suggested, and is made meaningful, by associations with the buildings' purposes. It is not always so. For Ogaan, an exclusive boutique situated in Hauz Khas in New Delhi, Vasant and Revathi Kamath replicated the forms and materials of mud architecture, thus creating a nostalgic evocation of village India as a context for the sale of *haute couture* to sophisticated urban dwellers. Such criticism might be thought heavy-handed: the

116 SCOPE Office complex, New Delhi, by Raj Rewal, 1980s.

117 Recycling the massing of Rajasthani housing: a school building for the French Embassy, New Delhi, by Raj Rewal, 1980s.

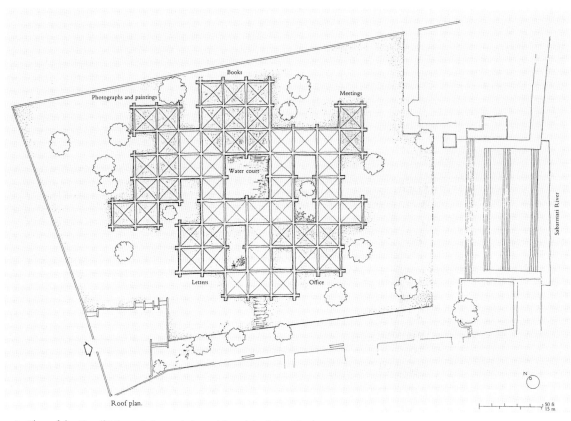

Photographs and paintings · Books · Meetings

Water court

Letters · Office

Sabarmati River

N

Roof plan.

50 ft
15 m

118 Plan of the Gandhi Smarak Sangrahalaya, Ahmadabad, by Charles Correa, 1958.

reference is clearly intended to be playful. But this defence merely highlights the problem: the use of rural forms and materials in an urban context necessarily renders them unserious, turning the lives of the rural poor into a whimsical game for the élite, in the manner of Marie Antoinette. In Jaipur, the nearest equivalent of Ogaan is Chokhi Dhani, a mud village air-conditioned restaurant on the Sanganer road.

A second approach to the problem of regional identity – even more directly relevant to our subject – has been the use of selected elements of *vastu vidya*, in particular its vocabulary and its salient forms. On the part of those who have taken this path, this has not been an attempt to place

architectural design within a fully revived system of *vastu vidya*; it has been the insertion of parts of that system into the repertoire of Modern architecture. It was again Charles Correa who pioneered the use of the *vastu purusha mandala* in this manner. He has employed this motif in several designs; most famously in the Jawahar Kala Kendra in Jaipur (1986), described in Chapter Five. The point that bears repeating is that in this project there has been no attempt to employ the principles of the *mandala*, only its configuration; and all of the related elements of *vastu vidya* are ignored (in spite of the use of Sanskritic vocabulary in its public presentation). To say this is not to deny to Correa, as an independent and original architect, the right to make whatever

119 The street front of the temple complex.

120 Part of the east or temple side of the central courtyard.

121 Detail of the west or entrance side of the central courtyard,
showing the dado and (left) the central entrance.

122 Back wall of the northern range of the courtyard.

123 Detail of the front of the Albert Hall.

124 The *chhatri* of Maharaja Sawai Jai Singh II at Gaitor, with the identical
chhatri of Maharaja Sawai Ram Singh II partly obscured behind.

125 The Rajendra Pol, Jaipur City Palace, by the office of Chiman Lal, 1900.

126 The upper balcony of the Mubarak Mahal.

127 The Rambagh
Palace, Jaipur,
remodelled by Swinton
Jacob, Chiman Lal and
Bhola Nath, 1909–16, and
later extended.

128 The Rambagh
Palace, detail of the
veranda.

129 New housing in Vidyadhar Nagar, after designs by B. V. Doshi.

130 Jawahar Kala Kendra, Jaipur, by Charles Correa.

use of architectural history appeals to his creative imagination and to his clients; it is merely to point out that he has exerted that right. The design of the Jawahar Kala Kendra *refers* to *vastu vidya*; but it does not *embody* it. To employ a distinction promoted by Correa himself, one might say that the imposition of the *mandala* as a strictly geometric ground plan makes the design a 'transfer' of the past, where the use of its principles could have been a 'transformation'. B. V. Doshi's design for Vidyadhar Nagar (1985) makes an analogous gesture: though the eighteenth-century plan of Jaipur is reproduced and elaborated as a unit of composition, no use is made of its organizing logic.

Although they have been the most inventive, Doshi and Correa have not been the only architects to adopt the *mandala* as an indigenizing device. The *mandala* is also found in the work of otherwise very different architects, such as D. K. Bubbar. Whatever their differences, however, these architects are united in employing the *mandala* as a theme rather than as one element in an integrated design approach. Where once it was a logic, the *mandala* has become a topic. If the attempt was to avoid visual pastiche, by invoking an indigenous feature which related to the plan rather than to structural or ornamental forms, the result is not wholly successful, since the use is still decontextualized. In place of visual pastiche we have a conceptual pastiche.[12]

So, just as a Post-Modern architect operating in, for example, Japan would typically acquaint himself with local historical forms in order to enliven his design with a recognizably Japanese theme, so architects in India have turned to their own indigenous traditions. For the most part (though not in every case) reluctant to deploy historical forms such as *chhatris*, domes and *jharokhas*, in the manner of the Indo-Saracenic architects, they have sought other kinds of reference. Village India and *vastu vidya* particularly recommend themselves as points of refuge in this quest; the first because, as a living tradition, it can be seen as indigenous without belonging exclusively to the past, the second because it is a theory not a style. But in each case their partial use turns them from a method into an embellishment, a form of pastiche not far removed, after all, from that of the Indo-Saracenic movement.

THE *vastu* CONSULTANTS

Intellectually very far removed from the world of professional architects, but now engaged in an uneasy tangle with them, is a new class of *Vastu* consultant. These are people who may have some, or little, or no knowledge of either architecture or engineering, and who present themselves as authorities on *vastu shastra* (though they vary too in their degree of acquaintance with the texts). They advise their clients chiefly on matters of orientation and internal organization of houses and places of work such as factories, seeking to persuade them that correct adherence to *Vastu* principles in such matters will ensure happiness or prosperity, while their violation will be ruinous.[13] For the clients this advice is a quite separate matter from the actual process of building, which is entrusted still to the architect or engineer. Often the two professions operate antagonistically. Concerned almost exclusively with issues of orientation, the *Vastu* consultant is little interested in the architectural envelope, and is not constrained to work out how his prescriptions can be accommodated in practice; while the architect, who may have little or no sympathy for the consultant's arcane ideas, may resent the limitations they impose upon his design and so consider him an unwelcome interference.

If the architects' own appeals to *vastu vidya* are selective and fragmentary, so too in different ways are those of the *Vastu* consultants, who are to be distinguished from the traditional *vastu shastris*, learned in all aspects of building design. The consultants' emphasis on orientation principles, at the expense of the wider range of issues that *vastu vidya* addresses, throws the whole system off balance. Certainly, within conventional *vastu vidya* the orientation principles are a crucial component, but they are only one component, which interacts with all the others. And they were never a set of inflexible rules governing where various functions should be located, but rather (like the *mandala*, with which they co-operate) a versatile conceptual framework within which the actualities of any given project could be resolved. The tendency amongst the ever growing band of consultants is to reduce *vastu vidya* to a set of neat programmatic prescriptions, which can work against, not as a part of, the building process.

If *vastu vidya* is identified with this reduced version (and increasingly it is), then it becomes easier for architects and some observers to dismiss it as superstitious nonsense, harder for them to respect it as a viable system. For many now *vastu vidya* is perceived as offering a short cut to wealth and happiness through an appropriate alignment of walls, doors and furniture. Such a perception may enhance its appeal to some, but for others – including the majority of architects – it merely reinforces the prejudice that *vastu vidya* is the domain of confidence tricksters and the gullible.

Ironically, architects have contributed much towards assisting the consultants to establish their niche by failing to satisfy all the requirements of the client. The Indian businessman, engaged on a daily basis with modern industrial technology, international standards and perhaps also foreign markets, experiences a sense of rapid change and uprootedness, of severance from the business world of his forebears; and the modern factory and house, however well adapted to his practical needs, do nothing to soothe this disjunction, to communicate enduring values. The *Vastu* consultant offers him a sense of connection – and increased profits to boot. Engaging a consultant as well as an architect adds a missing layer of meaning to the work place and the home. Following certain Modernist nostrums, there has been a fashion amongst some architects to speak of the structure and the spirit of architecture as discrete elements (a separation that would be meaningless within conventional *vastu vidya*); and so it is hardly surprising – even if it is regrettable – that others on occasion succeed in colonizing the element of spirit.

The travesty of *vastu vidya* currently practised by the consultants reintroduces an aspect of the system into architecture, but imbalanced as it is it cannot be considered a revival; and it is the chief cause of the continuing alienation of *vastu vidya* from the mainstream of the architectural profession.

THE CRAFTSMEN

Across India, craftsmen remain a repository not only of traditional technical skills but also to some degree of knowledge about *vastu vidya*. Numerically they are considerably reduced in comparison with the situation observed by Gordon Sanderson 90 years ago, as their opportunities for employment have continued to diminish. Craftsmen are engaged in conservation programmes by the Archaeological Survey of India and by private sponsors. They are not generally engaged alongside architects on new projects, except to produce off-the-peg fragments of traditional architecture, such as *jalis*, with which some projects (notably hotels) are embellished and Indianized. Mostly excluded as designers from the building site, they are frequently demoralized, though some still perceive themselves as the guardians of *vastu vidya*, and in some instances are the literal guardians of little-known *vastu shastras*.

There have been a few isolated initiatives to relieve their situation. One in Jaipur was the short-lived Institute of Traditional Building Arts, directed by P. K. Jain. Established by the Government of Rajasthan, this institute enabled selected craftsmen to practise and develop their skills, mostly on state-sponsored conservation projects. Even here, however, there was little co-operation with architects, and it did not serve to bring craft skills back into the larger domain of building design. The modern working methods of the architects leave little scope for collaboration with craftsmen in the design, and few architects are prepared to surrender any share of the responsibility that their profession has won for them. Furthermore, in spite of a prevailing sentimentality about craft skills, many contemporary architects – like their colonial predecessors – remain sceptical about the competence of people with little formal education, unable to communicate in English or standard Hindi. Where they do work together, as on some conservation programmes, the wide divergences in vocabulary, methods and aesthetics can lead to mutual incomprehension and so to a stiffening rather than a resolution of entrenched positions. Given opportunities to work alone, some master craftsmen – such as Premji Mistri of Amber – are capable of producing complex and successful buildings operating through a traditional system of *vastu vidya*.

Potential

If *vastu vidya* can still be relevant to architecture in India, it is surely not as a thematic device in Modern design, nor as an arcane vocabulary for the presentation of a project, nor as a piece of mumbo-jumbo with which to terrorize householders and businessmen in their pursuit of security. Instead it has a potential role as a structuring logic for architectural design, as in the example of the Ramachandra Temple. That *vastu vidya* is capable of serving as a paradigm for new design becomes clear as soon as some of the common objections to it are addressed.

vastu vidya IS NOT A STYLE

It is important to emphasize that a renewed use of *vastu vidya* need not entail the revival of a particular – or indeed any – historical style. *Vastu vidya* is not archaic, nor does it favour any particular formal vocabularies. In the first place, the texts of *vastu vidya* do not alone – without the accompanying practise – generate any given style. Some texts, to be sure, name and discuss a particular regional style;[14] but without the corresponding buildings the style could not be deduced or recreated from the text alone. Each of the texts presupposes that the architect is working within a given architectural language; it does not create such a language. As a matter of fact, a text could not do so if it tried: being made of words, a text can only tell, it cannot show; if it seeks to specify a visual language it can do so only by pointing to one already existing in the architectural record. Texts, then, do not make styles, they presuppose them; and which visual language is employed depends on the prevailing fashion.

It is the logic that is paramount, not the forms. Any given set of forms can be submitted to this logic or rigour. This is why it is possible, for example, for the Ramachandra Temple and medieval temples to look so different from each other while both adhering to the same tradition of *vastu* principles. The visual language of each relates to the architectural developments of its own time and place, and this accounts for their differences. And of course examples could be multiplied: historical buildings across India reveal immense stylistic diversities, as different regional and temporal forms developed within the common discipline.

The Ramachandra Temple is just one example of a successful design arising out of adherence to *vastu vidya* principles at a given time and place. It is the adherence that is worthy of imitation, not the style that happened then to prevail. The key factor is the method, not the form.

WHY IS *vastu vidya* NEEDED?

In its manifestoes and early manifestations the Modern Movement appeared to offer a new and vitalizing logic, not only for architecture but for society itself. It is no longer controversial to say that the promise has not been fulfilled. At one level (and the charge may seem curiously reminiscent of a standard objection to *vastu vidya*), Modernism's programme was too general, too universal and ideal; the solutions it offered were too uniform and unyielding, taking insufficient account of regional diversity and culture. This led to a sense of alienation, particularly amongst the public, and it is one of the major factors behind the prevailing disillusionment with Modernist architecture. At another level, and perhaps contradictorily, as it is practised today, including in India, Modernism and its Post-Modern derivatives seem to lack any recognizable logic at all. Or rather, the structuring logic of any given building emerges from the exigencies

and constraints of that particular project, in isolation. The architect and his team have to develop a structuring logic for each and every project; and although this logic may then be patiently explained to the patron, and to the readers of international architectural journals, it does not readily communicate itself to the building's users, who are again left baffled and alienated. So, the concept for the design, developed uniquely for the purpose in hand, is not accessible to the public, for whom the design may therefore appear arbitrary or meaningless, except at the level of its internationalism – expressed most powerfully through the materials and the aesthetic – where what it communicates is coercive and soulless.

Vastu vidya is an alternative structuring logic that, within an Indian context, avoids both these problems. Regionally specific, it avoids universal abstractions; culturally shared, it is a system in which both architect and user start from the same position of understanding. Tied to other systems of thought within the Indian cultural context, it can function as a framework of communication, a language common to the architect and the user. For although, as we have shown, the formerly widespread understanding of the system has been much damaged in recent history, there is fertile ground for new growth. The current fragmentary uses of *vastu vidya*, however misguided, serve at least to demonstrate a vast public interest.

Modernism and Post-Modernism enable an architect to communicate to the user on one level about a global culture (about which the user may well be ambivalent), and on another level about himself (which may, in truth, be of little interest). Neither of these extremes creates in the mind of the disoriented user any significant sense of society. The Post-Modernist's appeal to regional values is all too often intentionally superficial and restricted:

it is about selecting from the heritage elements that can be refashioned into an easily recognizable, and marketable, personal idiom, about promoting the individual architect as a brand name. *Vastu vidya* by contrast is a language to which both architect and user stand in the same relationship. It offers the architect a paradigm or discipline for his design which can be readily understood by the user; it offers the user a context for approaching a building at meaningful levels of generality and specificity. *Vastu vidya* tends to promote architecture that is anonymous, where self-expression is not central. It may be hard now to persuade celebrated architects of the virtues of anonymity, of a lessening of the professional ego. It would notbe so hard, one suspects, to persuade their clients. Anonymity has become an underrated virtue.

IS *vastu vidya* TRUE?

In the relevant *shastras*, some of the principles of *vastu vidya* are bolstered by what may be read as promises or threats regarding the consequences of observing or violating them. For some current users this is a large part of their appeal: they hope that restructuring the home or workplace according to *vastu* principles will bring happiness or success, or reverse ill fortune. Equally, this aspect generates a deal of scepticism amongst other observers, including many architects, who seize on it as a reason to dismiss the whole of *vastu vidya* as fraudulent. Both sceptics and believers, though, are motivated to ask the same question: is *vastu vidya* true? Can anyone demonstrate that what the *shastras* have to say about the consequences of applying or ignoring it is valid? Such questions are based on a misunderstanding of the nature and purposes of *vastu vidya*; indeed, both scepticism and belief are equally inappropriate as stances towards it.

The primary purpose of adhering to a principle of *vastu vidya* is that it exists as a principle. Together the principles amount to a discipline that has been widely understood, and thus renders an architectural design intelligible. Some analogies suggest themselves here, which are worth exploring briefly because, though none is exact and they all have weaknesses, the correspondences with, and distinctions from, other systems, are instructive.

The first analogy is with music. Within Indian classical music, certain conventions govern the formation of a *raga*. No one asks whether these conventions have any truth content; the question would be meaningless. All accept that the musician wishing to compose a *raga* must understand and work within the discipline of the conventions. An accomplished musician can stretch and adapt them; indeed that is how classical music develops over time. But broadly the conventions are accepted willingly because they define the form of the *raga*. If a musician rejects them outright, he is not composing a *raga*: his audience will not be able to recognize his performance as a *raga*. Similarly, the rules of a game such as chess exist to structure the game. They are neither true nor false, simply rules. Each player acts individually within their structure. If one player breaks the rules he has ceased to play the game; he has stepped outside a contract made with his opponent, who will therefore be unable to continue to play with him. The strength of these two analogies is that they indicate that the main purpose of the principles of *vastu vidya* is not to deliver wealth and happiness but to establish a system that allows for communication, for mutual comprehension, in an action. The *vastu vidya* architect enters into a contract of understanding with the user, just as a musician does with his audience, or a chess player with his opponent. The weakness of these analogies is that the conventions of music and of chess are closed systems, making no claim to a relationship with other fields of activity, or with life. Some of the principles of *vastu vidya*, by contrast, do correspond with other systems, including *jyotish vidya* and *ayurveda*. Indeed it is on such correspondences that its power to communicate partly depends.

A further analogy might be made with certain kinds of religious law, such as those governing diet, or regulations regarding the performance of rituals. Where such regulations are accepted by those within the system, they are accepted firstly because they give physical form to religious ideas. Such practices are widely recognized conventions that the individual chooses to accept and apply. Of course, more might be said here about the meanings and efficacy of ritual actions;[15] but the weakness of this analogy lies in the fact – and it is one that needs stressing – that *vastu vidya* is not a religion. It is true that the *vastu shastras* are composed within the context of a religious tradition (they standardly begin, for example, with a sacred invocation), and some of their principles (such as the primacy of the *brahmasthana*) relate to religious ideas, but the same might be said of texts about music. Following the principles of *vastu vidya* is not in itself a type of religious observance. It is important to emphasize this in the current climate, as Indic ideas are today being promoted by some as part of a Hindu chauvinist agenda. At all levels of Indian society there are those who seek to fabricate a Hindu identity in political opposition to foreign influences and to the region's religious minorities. The activities of the *Vastu* consultants are susceptible to hijacking for such purposes, but the practice of a properly understood *vastu vidya* does not contribute to that agenda any more than does the enjoyment of Indian music.

Asking whether *vastu vidya* is true presupposes an identification between *vastu vidya* and only one aspect of its orientation principles. This caricatures *vastu vidya* and mistakes its purpose – not a sound basis on which either to accept or to dismiss it. The principal aim of *vastu vidya* is not to generate wealth but to generate architecture. It should go without saying that fine architecture can be more conducive to personal felicity than bad architecture.

A final analogy may be helpful. Traditional Indian cuisine promotes certain combinations of ingredients and methods for preparing them. These ideas relate to other systems of Indian thought, notably *ayurveda*. But to suppose that good health was the primary aim of *pak vidya* would be to miss all its subtlety: a healthy diet is not the aim but the lowest common denominator of any system of cooking; no one would seriously propose a system that ignored food's life-sustaining properties. The point of *pak vidya* is to move beyond that base to explore the ways in which food can not only sustain but enhance life. To suppose that all its ideas ultimately have a medical basis would be severely reductionist, to take a utilitarian view of a delightful art. Similarly, *vastu vidya*, taken as a whole and not selectively, is as complex and elaborate as it is precisely because it addresses every aspect of a developed and refined art.

SCIENTIFIC VALIDATION

This last analogy introduces a related problem. Amongst the current enthusiasts of *vastu vidya*, including some *Vastu* consultants, there has arisen a quest for scientific validation. This phrase is intended to describe the efforts by some to reinforce or rationalize the ideas of *vastu vidya* by arguing that an independent, scientific analysis would arrive at the same results by different means. This is a way of saying that the manner in which *vastu vidya* encourages us to build is demonstrably beneficial in terms of health, by some objective and external test. Standard techniques involve talk of climate control or sanitation or engaging energy lines. Such an approach was implicit in aspects of the rationalization offered by P. K. Acharya, and it has been adopted more recently and explicitly by others, including members of the Sri Aurobindo Ashram Centre for Scientific Research at Pondicherry.

The impetus behind this effort is to find a justification sufficient to convince themselves, their clients, and sometimes also doubting architects, to offer an affirmative answer to the nagging question 'Is *vastu vidya* valid?' At one level it could be said that the success of their endeavour will depend on the authority of their scientific methods, and ironically there is some risk that this particular appeal to science will alienate rather than appease many of a scientific mind.

More importantly, perhaps, the endeavour itself is, once again, mistaken, because it ignores the terms in which the *shastras* themselves rationalize their ideas – a curious way to respect the tradition. To seek scientific validation is to imply that the *vastu shastris* of the past arrived at their ideas by some concealed empirical means, and then rationalized them in the ways they did because these were the only methods available to them; and that it is open to us, in view of our more advanced scientific understanding, to rediscover the 'real' origin. This approach is used to justify evading the texts' own accounts of their reasoning, as well as much of their potentially inconvenient detail; and the New Age *Vastu* expert is left free to focus on a supposedly scientific core. This seems to us an inadmissible way of characterizing the relationship between past and present: it projects a past cleverer than it knew, regrettably wrapped in superstition, helped by and helping an all-seeing present. The

scientific validators' attempted manoeuvre is to elude the convention and grasp the central reality. Our view is that the convention is the point to grasp, that the convention and the reality are one and the same.

DISCREPANT TEXTS

A recognition that it is the convention that is the core to grasp also helps resolve another common difficulty. Within the field of *vastu vidya* it has to be acknowledged that there are frequently discrepancies between different texts or practitioners on certain ideas. One may positively affirm one regulation, another something slightly different, and a third something entirely contradictory. Sometimes even a single text or practitioner can be self-contradictory. These problems might mislead would-be practitioners to ask which text should be privileged, which has greater authority or authenticity, and which is correct.

Like the exercise in scientific validation, such questions presuppose the existence of a central or transcendent reality, a single 'correct' *vidya*, of which the texts are all imperfect reflections. That would be a mistaken assumption, for there is no one definitive *vastu vidya*, no central reality, but only a tradition of knowledge. And the purpose of a regulation is not to reveal or give access to some absolute reality, but to be a regulation. It does not much matter ultimately which version of the regulations is adhered to – though some versions may be more appropriate in given places and times, having been developed with those contexts in view. Indeed the discrepancies can be explained historically: they arose because various texts were composed in different places and times, by authors with differing expertise and audiences, with more or less knowledge of preceding texts, or with a view to different local conditions. The presence of discrepancies does not invalidate the regulations, because the regulations require no validation beyond their status as such. Indeed, they are not so much discrepancies as variations that indicate the living nature of the tradition. If all texts said precisely the same thing, there would have been no need for more than one version; their variety is a sign of the continuing adaptability of the shared tradition.

CONCLUSION

The original purpose and value of *vastu vidya* was to provide a guiding logic for architectural design, a discipline or system within which to structure the design process. The example of Jaipur shows how such a system operates in practice, as well as demonstrating the system's flexibility. The case study of the Ramachandra Temple illustrates the functioning of *vastu vidya* in a period of rapid economic, social and political change, a period in these respects analogous to our own. The building's multi-functional nature and complex character further demonstrate that *vastu vidya* is not restricted to one domain or type.

From this adaptability and openness to change, it is evident that the use of *vastu vidya* today would not entail a return to the past. *Vastu vidya* is a living, evolving system, able to serve the needs of our own era, not a refuge from contemporary life. Its application is therefore neither regressive nor conservative. It might justly be called 'classical', in the sense that it places a set of culturally agreed, widely understood norms at the centre of the creative process. In this sense too its use is demotic and anti-élitist: in contrast to the Post-Modernist's exclusion of all but *aficionados* from the charmed circle of comprehension, it satisfies the need for

societal participation in architectural understanding.

The way ahead lies on two fronts – the theoretical and the practical – which, as ever, should go hand in hand. There is a need for further research and for the wider dissemination of knowledge about *vastu vidya*: although once widely understood, it has become a comparatively obscure element of the Indian tradition, and this situation needs to be reversed, for example through the schools of architecture. There is ample evidence of a public appetite for such knowledge. But research into the past needs to be based on an analysis of texts and of extant buildings, rather than on phoney scientific speculations. There is also a need for a theoretical expansion of *vastu vidya*: just as throughout its past it constantly evolved and adapted to changing conditions, so thought needs to be given today to the integration into the system of new materials and techniques.

The renewed application of *vastu vidya* in building projects should be simultaneous. In today's varied context it could not be proposed as the only valid system for future design, but as one worth reinvestigating, especially since others have demonstrably failed. In particular, other approaches to the re-establishment of a regional identity, operating within the paradigm of Modernism, have delivered only new forms of pastiche. *Vastu vidya* would be more successful in meeting this need, because of its power to function as a method of communication between architects and users. One aspect that is likely to distinguish any such projects, above and beyond the inventive use of a rigorous discipline, is the reintroduction of high-quality craftsmanship in the treatment of materials, not least because of the necessary dependence on craftsmen as guardians of the practical knowledge of *vastu vidya*.

In other spheres of India's cultural life today – in dress, cuisine, music and dance, for example –

traditional systems have survived the vicissitudes of
history and continue to evolve as vigorous
expressions of regional identity. No one doubts
their validity in the modern age; much less would
anyone propose abandoning them as archaic. On
the contrary, they are cherished, when they are not
taken for granted, as ingredients of a living culture.
In this wider context, architecture stands out as an
exception. In architecture, a gulf divides current
practice from the heritage, and the attempts to
bridge it have not carried conviction. The reasons
for that gulf lie, as we have shown, in the building
policies of successive periods since the mid-
nineteenth century, and most particularly in the dis-
engagement from indigenous architectural theory.
It is through a re-engagement with that theory,
therefore, that we may reach a remedy.

References

1 CONCEPTUAL CITIES

1 *Sukraniti* I. 41–4 (B. K. Sarkar, trans., *The Sukraniti*, repr. New Delhi, 1975, pp. 5–6).

2 Although at least one authority (Lallanji Gopal, *The Sukraniti: A Nineteenth-century Text*, Benares, 1978, places the *Sukraniti* as late as the nineteenth century, others have offered various dates, mostly from AD 700 onwards. In the present context this dispute is of little importance, since a part of the case being made is that all such treatises draw on an inherited body of knowledge.

3 See, for example, *Manusmriti* VII. 5–8 (Wendy Doniger, trans., *The Laws of Manu*, London, 1991, p. 128).

4 *Sukraniti* I. 245–8 (Sarkar, 1975, pp. 18–19).

5 *Sukraniti* I. 260–9 (Sarkar, 1975, p. 19).

6 *Sukraniti* I. 295–7, 740–1, II. 246–50 (Sarkar, 1975, pp. 21, 50, 76).

7 *Manasara* XLI. 48–9 (P. K. Acharya, trans., *Architecture of Manasara*, Allahabad, 1934, p. 435). Again this text is of uncertain date, though definitely not modern and probably of the Gupta period.

8 *Manasara* XLII. 2–74 (Acharya, 1934, pp. 436–40).

9 *Arthashastra* VI. 2. 33 (R. P. Kangle, trans., *The Kautilya Arthashastra*, repr. Delhi, 1972, p. 319). The text is datable to the Mauryan period.

10 *Arthashastra* VII. 1. 2 (Kangle, 1972, p. 321); *Manusmriti* VII. 160 (Doniger, 1991, p. 145). The *Manusmriti* or 'Laws of Manu' is a work of jurisprudence, dating from about the first century AD.

11 *Arthashastra* VI. 1. 1 (Kangle, 1972, p. 314); *Manusmriti* IX. 294 (Doniger, 1991, p. 229).

12 The *Aparajita Priccha* is a text of the twelfth or thirteenth century; see Lal Mani Dubey, *Aparajita Prccha: A Critical Study*, Allahabad, 1987, pp. 78–9. The *Rajavallabha* of Mandan is a fifteenth-century work; see V. 1–6 (Ramyatna Ojha, trans., *Vasturajavallabha of Mandana Sutradhara*, 2nd edn, Benares, 1934, pp. 53–5).

13 *Manasara* X. 39–87 (Acharya, 1934, pp. 95–7); *Mayamata* X. 5–36 (Bruno Dagens, trans., *Mayamatam: Treatise of Housing, Architecture and Iconography*, 2 vols, New Delhi, 1994, vol. I, pp. 89–97). A different list is given by *Samrangana Sutradhara* xxii. 2–7 (D. N. Shukla, trans., *Samarangana Sutradhara*, Delhi, 1994, p. 99).

14 *Manasara* IV, VIII (Acharya, 1934, pp. 13–14, 59–62); *Mayamata* IV, VIII (Dagens, 1994, vol. I, pp. 17–21, 51–5); *Samrangana Sutradhara* XVIII. 1–28 (Shukla, 1994, pp. 81–3); *Rajavallabha* II. 2 (Ojha, 1934, p. 17); *Vishvakarma Prakash* V. 1–183 (Pandit Mihirchand, trans., *Vishvakarma Prakash*, Bombay, 1988, pp. 33–46).

15 E.g. *Manasara* VII (Acharya, 1934, pp. 33–57); *Mayamata* VII (Dagens, 1994, vol. I, pp. 37–49).

16 *Mayamata* X. 16–17 (Dagens, 1994, vol. I, p. 93).

17 *Manasara* X. 110–14 (Acharya, 1934, p. 98).

18 *Samrangana Sutradhara* XXIII. 2–4 (Shukla, 1994, p. 103); *Rajavallabha* II. 4 (Ojha, 1934, p. 18).

19 *Mayamata* X. 18 (Dagens, 1994, vol. I, p. 93). A *danda* (rod) is a unit of measurement roughly equivalent to 2 m.

20 See, for example, *Samrangana Sutradhara* XXIII. 5–8 (Shukla, 1994, p. 103).

21 *Arthashastra* II. 36. 26–8 (Kangle, 1972, pp. 186–7). See also II. 4. 1 (Kangle, p. 67).

22 *Sukraniti* I. 601–2 (Sarkar, 1975, p. 40). See also I. 519–22 (Sarkar, p. 34).

23 *Arthashastra* II. 4. 17 (Kangle, 1972, p. 70); *Sukraniti* IV. 4. 132–3, 405–12 (Sarkar, 1975, pp. 166, 182).

24 *Manasara* IX. 383–98, X. 44–7 (Acharya, 1934, pp. 84, 95).

25 *Rajavallabha* IV. 12 (Ojha, 1934, p.41; *Samrangana Sutradhara* XXIII. 124–5 (Shukla, 1994, p. 111) suggests, however, that the last problem can be overcome by painting an image of the deity on the temple's rear wall.

26 *Samrangana Sutradhara* XXIII. 88–103 (Shukla, 1994, pp. 108–9). The same distribution is given by *Arthashastra* II. 4. 8–15 (Kangle, 1972, pp. 68–9). An alternative pattern follows the same sequence of castes but starts with the east (for Brahmins) and ends with the north; see, for example, *Rajavallabha* IV. 18–20 (Ojha, 1934, p. 42–3).

27 *Samrangana Sutradhara* XXIII. 88–103 (Shukla, 1994, pp.

108–9); *Arthashastra* II. 4. 8 and 12 (Kangle, 1972, pp. 68–9); *Rajavallabha* IV. 18–20 (Ojha, 1934, pp. 42–3).

28 E.g. *Mayamata* X. 77–87 (Dagens, 1994, vol. I, pp. 107–9).

29 E.g. *Mayamata* X. 86–7 (Dagens, 1994, vol. I, p. 109).

30 *Mayamata* XXIX. 1–3 (Dagens, 1994, vol. II, p. 623); see also *Manasara* X. 44–7 (Acharya, 1934, p. 95).

31 *Manasara* XL. 38–48 (Acharya, 1934, p. 425).

32 *Manasara* XL. 73–157 (Acharya, 1934, pp. 427–31).

33 Cf. *Mayamata* XXIX. 30–64 (Dagens, 1994, vol. II, pp. 631–9).

34 E.g. *Mayamata* X. 21–6, XXIX. 158 (Dagens, 1994, vol. I, pp. 93–5, vol. II, p. 661).

35 The text is the *Kurmvilas* of Dulichand, a fragment of which is included in G. N. Bahura, ed., *Sawai Jai Singh Charit by Kavi Atmaram* (Jaipur, 1979), p. 81.

36 *Ramayana* VII, *chaupai* 25, *chhand* 8 (F. S. Growse, trans., *The Ramayana of Tulsidas*, repr. Delhi, 1978, pp. 646–7).

37 *Ramayana* I, *chaupai* 210, *doha* 213, *chaupai* 211 (Growse, 1978, pp. 134–5).

2 A TIME AND A PLACE

1 M. L. Sharma, *A History of the Jaipur State* (Jaipur, 1969), pp. 39–44.

2 See the letters exchanged between Aurangzeb and his son Mohammed Akbar, in Bisheshwar Nath Reu, *Glories of Marwar and the Glorious Rathors* (Jodhpur, 1943), Appx B6.

3 Ashim Kumar Roy, *History of the Jaipur City* (New Delhi, 1978), pp. 4–5. The major biography of Sawai Jai Singh II is V. S. Bhatnagar, *Life and Times of Sawai Jai Singh 1688 1743* (Delhi, 1974).

4 Gopal Narayan Bahura, *Literary Heritage of the Rulers of Amber and Jaipur* (Jaipur, 1976), p. 13; Robert W. Stern, *The Cat and the Lion: Jaipur State and the British Raj* (Leiden, 1988), pp. 10–11.

5 Chandramani Singh, 'Costumes and Textiles', *Marg*, vol. XXX/4 (1977), p. 95.

6 Bahura, 1976, p. 53.

7 *Ramavilasa Kavyam*, *passim* (G. N. Bahura, ed., *Ramavilasakavyam by Vishwanath Bhatt C. Renade*, [Jaipur, 1978]); *Sawai Jai Singh Charit*, 392–9 (G. N. Bahura, ed., *Sawai Jai Singh Charita by Kavi Atmaram*, Jaipur, 1979, pp. 36–7, and note pp. 94–5). The later text is the *Ishvarvilasa Mahakavyam* of Krishna Bhatta: see A. K. Roy, 1978, p. 22.

8 The rite is described in the *Kurmvilas* of Dulichand, 75–90 (see Bahura, ed., 1979, pp. 82–4). It was performed in 1734 and repeated in 1742: see V. S. Bhatnagar in *Marg*, vol. XXX/ 4 (n.p.); and Bahura, ed., 1979, pp. 108, 146.

9 Roy, 1978, p. 26.

10 Roy, 1978, pp. 57–8.

11 Roy, 1978, p. 58; 1982, p. 47.

12 Roy, 1978, p. 51.

13 Jaipur *kapadwara* documents cited in Bahura, ed., 1979, pp. 140, 146.

14 *Sawai Jai Singh Charit*, 447 (Bahura, ed., 1979, p. 45). Roy (1978, p. 166) dates the founding of Jai Niwas to 1726.

15 Roy, 1978, p. 235 (line 183).

16 Bahura, 1976, p. 25; Roy, 1978, p. vii.

17 A. K. Roy, 'Town Planning in Jaipur', *Cultural Heritage of Jaipur*, ed. J. N. Asopa (Jaipur, 1982), p. 45.

18 E.g. Andreas Volwahsen, *Architecture of the World: India* (Lausanne, 1968), p. 87.

19 A. K. Roy, 'The Dream and the Plan', *Marg*, vol. XXX/4 (1977), p. 26; Roy, 1978, pp. xi, 35; Roy, 1982, p. 44. See also Yaduendra Sahai, 'Sawai Jai Singh: Patron of Architecture', *Cultural Heritage of Jaipur*, ed. J. N. Asopa (Jaipur, 1982), p. 31; Aman Nath, *Jaipur: The Last Destination* (Bombay, 1993), pp. 58–9. The role of the *shastras* is acknowledged by Volwahsen, 1968, p. 48. An agnostic stance is taken by George Michell, 'The Plan of Jaipur', *Storia della Città*, vol. V (1978), pp. 65, 67; and by Michael Carapetian, 'Jaipur: The Pink City', *The Architectural Review*, vol. CLXXII/1027 (1982), p. 36; and Joan L. Erdman, *Patrons and Performers in Rajasthan* (Delhi, 1985), p. 33; Erdman, 'Jaipur: City Planning in Eighteenth-century India', *Shastric Traditions in Indian Arts*, ed. Anna Libera Dallapiccola (Stuttgart, 1989), p. 223.

20 Sten Nilsson, 'Jaipur: In the Sign of Leo', *Magasin Tessin*, no. 1 (1987), pp. 12–14; Nilsson, 'Jaipur – Reflections of a Celestial Order', *Aspects of Conservation in Urban India*, ed. Sten Nilsson (Lund, 1995), pp. 110–11.

21 E.g., Roy, 1978, pp. xi, 31–2, 35; 1982, p. 43; Yaduendra Sahai, 'Pink City; Its Original Colour and Allied Problems', *Cultural Contours of India*, ed. Vijai Shankar Srivastava (New Delhi, 1981), p. 396.

22 See G.H.R. Tillotson, *The Rajput Palaces* (London, 1987), pp. 169–71.

23 E. B. Havell, *Indian Architecture*, 2nd edn (London, 1927), pp. 222–4; based on Ram Raz, *An Essay on the Architecture of the Hindus* (London, 1834), pl. xlv. The idea is accepted by B. L. Dhama, *A Guide to Jaipur and Amber*, 2nd edn (Jaipur, 1955), p. 5; and by Nilsson, 1987, p. 11; and Nilsson, 1995, p. 109. For Nilsson to agree that it is a *prastara* while rejecting any shastric origin – cf. note 20 above – is of course self-contradictory. Havell's suggestion has been previously rejected by A. K. Roy, 1977, pp. 25–6; and Roy, 1978, pp. xi, 37–8.

24 Cf. P. K. Acharya, *Architecture of Manasara* (Allahabad, 1934), pp. 85–7.

25 For a quite distinct use of the term *prastara*, in relation to the arrangement of house forms, see Vibhuti Chakrabarti, *Indian Architectural Theory* (London, 1998), pp. 156–63.

26 Nilsson, 1987, p. 73; 1995, pp. 111–12. See also Aman Nath, 1993, p. 63.

27 Nilsson (1987, p. 17) specifies as the model Erlangen, as depicted in the *Grosser Atlas* published in Nuremberg in 1725, a copy of which is contained in the Jaipur palace *pothikhana*. But Susan Gole (*Indian Maps and Plans*, New Delhi, 1989, p. 44) has shown that this volume was acquired only after the construction of the city. It may be added that the only common feature between Jaipur and Erlangen (as depicted there) is once again the use of a grid. The Jesuit connection with Jaipur, discussed below, began in 1731.

28 Roy, 1978, p. 41; Carapetian, 1982, p. 36; Nilsson, 1987, p. 9.

29 Roy, 1978, pp. 41–3, 52, 58, 235.

30 Roy, 1978, p. 240; 1982, p. 45.

31 Roy, 1978, pp. 42–3.

32 Roy, 1978, p. 240. See also the reference to Vidyadhar's role as an elder statesman in 1750, in Sir Jadunath Sarkar, *Fall of the Mughal Empire*, vol. 1 (repr. New Delhi, 1997), p. 148.

33 This document is preserved in the Rajasthan State Archives, Bikaner; see Roy, 1978, pp. 52–3.

34 The plan is preserved in the Sawai Man Singh II Museum, Jaipur; cat. LS/14.

35 Cf. Roy, 1978, p. 39. Elswhere (Roy, 1982, p. 46) Roy reads the date on its reverse side as 1725, and proposes that building may have begun before the religious foundation ceremony – a most unlikely sequence of events.

36 Sawai Man Singh II Museum, Drawings Collection cat. nos 9 and 16; see also Gole, 1989, no. 108. These drawings are from the *pothikhana* collection; a further group of plans from the *kapadwara* are published in G. N. Bahura and Chandramani Singh, *Catalogue of Historical Documents in Kapad Dwara, Jaipur: Maps and Plans* (Jaipur, 1990).

37 For example, *Mayamata* X (Bruno Dagens, trans., *Mayamata: An Indian Treatise on Housing, Architecture and Iconography*, Delhi, 1985, p. 40).

38 Yaduendra Sahai, 1982, p. 32.

39 Joan Erdman, 1985, p. 35.

40 For the date of this temple, see Kesharlal Ajmera Jain and Jawaharlal Jain, eds, *The Jaipur Album* (Jaipur, 1935), chap. 17, p. 7f.

41 Sahai, 1982, p. 33; Erdman, 1989, p. 229. Roy (1978, p. 40) is more cautious.

42 E.g. Sawai Man Singh II Museum, Drawings Collection no. 16 (published in Gole, 1989, no. 108). This map exaggerates the width of the city to render the two half-wards equal in size to those on either side of them.

43 H. A. Newell, *Jaipur: The Astronomer's City* (London, 1915), p. 6; Roy, 1978, p. xi.

44 Volwahsen, 1968, p. 48.

45 Erdman, 1989, p. 229.

46 *Manasara* IX (Acharya, 1934, p. 87).

47 Gayatri Devi (*A Princess Remembers*, 3rd edn, Ghaziabad, 1983, p. 242) records that the original arrangement survived until independence.

48 Newell, 1915, p. 6; C.W. Waddington, *Indian India as Seen by a Guest in Rajasthan* (London, 1933), p. 101; Jain and Jain, eds, 1935, chap. 17, p. 2; Satish Davar, 'A Filigree City Spun out of Nothingness', *Marg*, vol. XXX/4 (1977), p. 57; Roy, 1978, p. viii; Jai Narayan Asopa, ed., *Cultural Heritage of Jaipur* (Jaipur, 1982), p. 26; Nilsson, 1987, p. 57; Erdman, 1989, p. 230.

49 The experiment is described in JSPWD report 1868, p. 7; Sahai, 1981, p. 398; Sahai, 1982, p. 34.

50 See also Dhama, 1955, pp. 19–20; Carapetian, 1982, p. 42.

51 E.g. JSPWD/Imarat reports 1884, p. 18 (for HRH the Duke of Connaught), and 1885, p. 6 (for the Viceroy, Lord Dufferin). The concomitant idea that pink is a traditional Rajasthani colour of welcome is wholly spurious: no such tradition is known to the citizens of Jaipur.

52 See Sahai, 1981, p. 397, and this article generally for a full discussion of the topic; also Nath, 1993, pp. 63–4.

53 For more on stones, see Sahai, 1981, pp. 396–7.

54 Roy, 1978, appx VI, no. 16.

55 Waddington, 1933, pp. 101–2. He may have miscounted the horses: Surya's chariot is conventionally drawn by seven.

56 Bahura, 1976, p. 33; Roy, 1978, pp. 161–2, 166. See also the accounts of the *murti*'s peregrinations given by R. Nath, M. Horstmann and G. N. Bahura, all in Margaret H. Case, ed., *Govindadeva: A Dialogue in Stone* (New Delhi, 1996), pp. 160–83, p. 186 and p. 205 respectively. The present temple is further discussed by C. Asher in Giles Tillotson, ed., *Stones in the Sand: The Architecture of Rajasthan* (Mumbai, 2001), pp. 68–77.

57 Sahai, 1982, p. 40.

58 Asopa, 1982, p. 91.

59 *Sawai Jai Singh Charit*, 452–3 (Bahura, ed., 1979, p. 46); Roy, 1978, p. 166; Asopa, ed., 1982, p. 91. The garden near Amber, which takes the name 'Kanak Vrindavan' from the original site of the *murti*, still exists. See also R. Nath in Case, ed., 1996, pp. 174–8.

60 Roy, 1978, pp. 160, 166. Roy also states that the hunting lodge was not established until 1726, but cf. note 14 above.

61 For example, *Manasara* X, 44–7 (Acharya, 1934, p. 95).

62 A. ff. Garrett and Chandrahar Guleri, *The Jaipur*

Observatory and its Builder (Allahabad, 1902), p. 14; Kaye, 1918, p. 53; Roy, 1978, pp. 16, 45; Erdman, 1985, p. 30.

63 *Sawai Jai Singh Charit*, 682 (Bahura, ed., 1979, p. 77 and note p. 104); Kaye, 1918, p. 46.

64 Roy, 1978, p. 228. For recent studies of the observatories, see also V. N. Sharma, *Sawai Jai Singh and his Observatories* (Jaipur, 1977) and Andreas Volwahsen, *Cosmic Architecture in India* (Munich, 2001).

65 Garrett and Guleri, 1902, p. 21.

66 Ibid., p. 15.

67 For connections between Jaipur and the Jesuits, see Gauvin Bailey, 'A Portuguese Doctor at the Maharaja of Jaipur's Court', *South Asian Studies*, vol. XI (1995), pp. 51–62.

68 Garrett and Guleri, 1902, pp. 66–7; Kaye, 1918, pp. 4, 90; Roy, 1978, p. 16.

69 For example, Davar, 1977, p. 39.

70 Nilsson, 1987, pp. 19–22; see also Nath, 1993, p. 66.

71 See Chakrabarti, 1998, pp. 43–53; and Vibhuti Chakrabarti, 'Orientation by Numbers: the Aya Formula of Indian Architectural Theory', *South Asian Studies*, vol. XVI (2000), pp. 45–54.

72 For an account of this context, see Tillotson, 1987.

73 For example, *Mayamata* XXIX (Dagens, 1985, pp. 261ff.).

74 It is exhibited in the corridor leading from the 'Sileh Khana' of the Museum.

75 For other accounts of the palace gates and their names, with some variations, see Newell, 1915, p. 9; Nath, 1993, p. 131. For an early, partial plan of the Chandra Mahal, see Bahura and Singh, 1990, no. 109, (p. 29 and fig. 39).

76 For example, *Mayamata* XXIX (Dagens, 1985, p. 267).

77 Rang Mahal and Shobha Nivas are alternative names for the same storey, not separate storeys as is usually suggested. The confusion arises because of the double height of the Sukh Nivas. Cf. Newell, 1915, p. 11; H. L. Showers, *Notes on Jaipur*, 2nd edn (Jaipur, 1916), pp.18–19; Nath, 1993, p. 143.

78 Roy, 1978, appx VI, no. 22, p. 229.

79 For example, *Mayamata* XXIX (Dagens, 1985, p. 260).

80 Louis Rousselet, *India and its Native Princes* (London, 1876), p. 226.

81 Now enclosed, this larger hall serves as the Art Gallery of the Museum. See Bahura and Singh, 1990, no. 13 (p. 18), which would indicate a late eighteenth–century date for this building. Ibid., no. 31 (p. 20 and fig. 14), labelled 'sarvato bhadra' does not in fact depict either palace structure.

82 *Pratap Prakash* (G. N. Bahura, ed., *Pratap Prakasa of Krishnadatta Kavi*, Jaipur, 1983, Introduction pp. 5–6 and text pp. 9–11).

83 Gole, 1989, notes on no. 108, p. 195, and 110, p. 197.

84 Maharaja Sawai Man Singh II Museum, Drawings Collection, no. 1, which is not included in Gole.

85 Bahura, 1976, pp. 73–4. On the Jaipur succession dispute, and the related dispute over Bundi, see also Sarkar, 1997, chaps 6 and 7.

86 Roy, 1978, appx VI, no. 31, p. 230.

87 Dhama, 1955, p. 50.

88 For a critique of its architectural quality, on grounds of diminished plasticity, see Tillotson, 1987, p. 183.

89 The phrase is here intended not to include Islamic, colonial and modern buildings.

3 THE COURTS OF RAMACHANDRA

1 Suha Ozkan in Aga Khan Award for Architecture, *Regionalism and Architecture* (Cambridge, 1985), pp. 13–14.

2 Doshi in ibid., p. 87.

3 A *hasta* is a unit of measurement equivalent to a person's forearm.

4 *Rajavallabha* V. 25 (Ramyatna Ojha, trans., *Vasturajavallabha of Mandana Sutradhara*, 2nd edn, Benares, 1934, p. 60); *Vishvakarma Prakash* VII. 56–66 (Pandit Mihirchand, trans., *Vishvakarmaprakash*, Bombay, 1988, pp. 65–66); *Samrangana Sutradhara* XXXV. 2–5 (D. N. Shukla, trans., *Samarangana Sutradhara*, Delhi, 1994, p. 174).

5 *Vishvakarma Prakash* VI. 61 (Mihirchand, 1988, p. 56); *Mayamata* XXVI. 196b (Bruno Dagens, trans., *Mayamatam: Treatise of Housing, Architecture and Iconography*, 2 vols, Delhi, 1994, vol. II, p. 563).

6 *Rajavallabha* IX. 30 (Ojha, 1934, p. 108); *Samrangana Sutradhara* XXIV.19–20 (Shukla, 1994, p. 116).

7 *Rajavallabha* V. 15 (Ojha, 1934, p. 56); *Samrangana Sutradhara* XXXII. 16–17 (Shukla, 1994, p. 164).

8 *Rajavallabha* V. 13 (Ojha, 1934, p. 56); *Samrangana Sutradhara* XXXII. 2–7 (Shukla, 1994, p. 163).

9 *Vishvakarma Prakash* VII. 83 (Mihirchand, 1988, p. 67).

10 *Samrangana Sutradhara* XXXII. 18 (Shukla, 1994, p. 164).

11 *Rajavallabha* IX. 17 (Ojha, 1934, pp. 104–5); the text mentions six, but appears to list seven materials.

12 Ibid., IX. 13 (Ojha, 1934, p. 104).

13 Ibid., IX. 38 (Ojha, 1934, p. 113).

14 *Vishvakarma Prakash* II. 116 (Mihirchand, 1988, p. 18).

15 For a full explanation of the *prastara* series, see Vibhuti Chakrabarti, *Indian Architectural Theory* (London, 1998), pp. 155–62.

16 *Samrangana Sutradhara* XXII. 20–29 and XXIV. 25–35 (Shukla, 1994, pp. 100, 116–7).

17 *Vishvakarma Prakash* II. 120 (Mihirchand, 1988, p. 18); *Samrangana Sutradhara* XXVII. 7 (Shukla, 1994, p. 138).

18 *Samrangana Sutradhara* XXIV. 25–35 (Shukla, 1994, pp. 16–7).

19 *Vishvakarma Prakash* II. 186 (Mihirchand, 1988, p. 23).

20 *Samrangana Sutradhara* XXX. 136–140 (Shukla, 1994, p. 157).

21 *Vishvakarma Prakash* XIII. 1–6 (Mihirchand, 1988, p. 93).

22 *Samrangana Sutradhara* XXVIII. 76 (Shukla, 1994, p. 191).

23 *Vishvakarma Prakash* VII. 101–103 (Mihirchand, 1988, p. 68).

24 *Rajavallabha* II. 19 (Ojha, 1934, p. 22).

25 Ibid., II. 13 (Ojha, 1934, p. 20).

26 *Vishvakarma Prakash* vii. 73 (Mihirchand, 1988, p. 67); this text also refers to the central courtyard as *garbha*.

27 Ibid., VI. 12 (Mihirchand, 1988, p. 52).

28 Ibid., VI. 56–61 (Mihirchand, 1988, pp. 55–6).

29 Ibid., I. 128 (Mihirchand, 1988, p. 72).

30 *Vishvakarma Prakash* VI. 6 (Mihirchand, 1988, p. 56); *Mayamata* XIX. 4–5 (Bruno Dagens, trans., *Mayamatam: Treatise of Housing, Architecture and Iconography*, 2 vols, New Delhi, 1994, vol. I, p. 307); *Prasad Mandan* III. 33 (Bhagvandas Jain, trans., *Sutradhar Mandan Virachit Prasad Mandan*, Jaipur, 1997, p. 56).

31 See Chapter Two, pp. 43–4.

4 RULES AND RULERS

1 Robert W. Stern, *The Cat and the Lion: Jaipur State in the British Raj* (Leiden, 1988), p. 1. For details of the similarly worded treaties with Udaipur and Bikaner (both also 1818), see James Tod, *Annals and Antiquities of Rajast'han*, 2 vols (repr., London, 1972), vol. I, p. 631; and K. K. Sehgal, *Bikaner* [Rajasthan District Gazetteers] (Jaipur, 1972), pp. 69–71.

2 Tod, vol. I, pp. xi, 524; vol. II, p. v.

3 G. N. Bahura, *Literary Heritage of the Rulers of Amber and Jaipur* (Jaipur, 1976), p. 85; G.C. Verma in Jai Narayan Asopa, ed., *Cultural Heritage of Jaipur* (Jaipur, 1982), p. 162.

4 It was transferred to new buildings outside the city walls in 1933; the temple complex facing the Hawa Mahal currently houses a middle school.

5 C. A. Baylay, 'Jaipur', *The Rajputana Gazetteer*, vol. II (Calcutta, 1879), p. 153; Kesharlal Ajmera Jain and Jawaharlal Jain, eds, *The Jaipur Album* (Jaipur, 1935), chap. vii, pp. 3–6; K. N. Shastry in Asopa, ed., 1982, pp. 179–80.

6 Bahura, 1976, p. 86.

7 *Jeypore State Public Works Reports* (JSPWD report) 1881, pp. 5–6; and H.B.W. Garrick, *Report of a Tour in the Punjab and Rajputana, 1883–84* (Calcutta, 1887), p. 3 (Garrick disapproved, judging the paving 'pretentious').

8 Yaduendra Sahai, 'Sawai Jai Singh, Patron of Architecture', in Asopa, ed., 1982, pp. 32–4. The present fountains are of course modern.

9 Bahura, 1976, p. 86.

10 H. L. Showers, *Notes on Jaipur*, 2nd edn (Jaipur, 1916), p. 32.

11 Opendro Nauth Sen, *Report on the Jaipur School of Arts* (Jaipur, 1878), p. 5.

12 Ibid., p. 1; see also Showers, 1916, p. 33.

13 Sen, 1878, p. 2; Showers, 1916, p. 34.

14 JSPWD report 1871, p. 5 and 1872, p. 1; Showers, 1916, p. 80.

15 Sen, 1878, p. 20.

16 See Thomas Holbein Hendley, *Memorials of the Jeypore Exhibition 1883* (Jaipur, 1893), p. viii and plate cxcv. The building is now known as the Maharaja Sawai Man Singh II Town Hall.

17 Ibid., p. v.

18 Ibid., p. v.

19 Thomas Holbein Hendley, *London Indo-Colonial Exhibition of 1886: Handbook of the Jeypore Courts* (Calcutta, 1886), p. 68.

20 Hendley, 1893; Sir Jadunath Sarkar, *A History of Jaipur c. 1503–1938* (Hyderabad, 1984), p. 367.

21 See Hendley, 1886.

22 JSPWD report 1876, pp. 2–3. The building's more famous namesake in London was, of course, named for the Prince's father, the Prince Consort. The Prince of Wales took the name Edward when he succeeded to the throne in 1901.

23 JSPWD report 1877, p. 3 and 1878, pp. 4–5.

24 JSPWD report 1874, p. 2 and 1876, pp. 1, 6.

25 JSPWD report 1879, p. 7. It has been suggested (Yaduendra Sahai, *Maharaja Sawai Ram Singh II of Jaipur: The Photographer Prince*, Jaipur, 1996, p. 45) that de Fabeck was removed from Jaipur in disgrace (though presumably any misdemeanour was not architectural).

26 JSPWD report 1881, p. 9.

27 For details of this lineage, see Raymond Callahan, 'Servants of the Raj: The Jacob Family in India', *Journal of the Society for Army Historical Research*, vol. LVI/225 (1978), pp. 4–24.

28 Hendley, 1886, p. 65; Showers, 1916, p. 67.

29 JSPWD report 1884, pp. 25, 78–9.

30 JSPWD report 1872, p. 1.

31 JSPWD report 1883, p. 19 and 1884, p. 15.

32 Jacob in Showers, 1916, p. 80 (for the attribution of the passage to Jacob, see ibid., preface).

33 Hendley, 1893, p. 55.

34 JSPWD report 1883, p. 3.

35 Sir Samuel Swinton Jacob, *The Jeypore Portfolio of Architectural Details*, 12 vols (London 1890–1913), vol. XI (1912), pl. 12.

36 Thomas Holbein Hendley, *Handbook of the Jeypore Museum* (Delhi, 1896), p. 1.

37 Ibid., p. 1

38 Jain and Jain, eds, 1935, chap. XVII, p. 7.

39 Hendley in Showers, 1916, pp. 29–30.

40 Jacob in Showers, 1916, p. 80.

41 Hendley, 1896, p. 2.

42 A similar process can be observed, even more polarized, in the making of the gate and screens for the Colonial and Indian Exhibition of 1886. The designs for the elevations were prepared by Jacob's office, but the ornamentation was carried out freely by Shekhavati wood-carvers. See JSPWD report 1885, p. 5; Hendley, 1886, p. 11; David Beevers, 'From the East Comes Light: A Relic of the Raj at Hove Museum', *The Royal Pavilion, Libraries and Museums Review* (July 2000), pp. 1–6.

43 Jacob, 1890–1913, vol. I, Preface.

44 See also the views of F. S. Growse and J. L. Kipling, described in G.H.R. Tillotson, *The Tradition of Indian Architecture* (London, 1989), pp. 84–92 and 98–102.

45 See, for example, Philip Davies, *Splendours of the Raj: British Architecture in India 1600–1947* (London, 1985), pp. 183–214; Thomas R. Metcalf, *An Imperial Vision: Indian Architecture and Britain's Raj* (London, 1989), pp. 55–140; Tillotson, 1989, pp. 46–56; and Christopher W. London, ed., *Architecture in Victorian and Edwardian India* (Bombay, 1994). For a particular study of the comparatively neglected figure of Vincent Esch, see G.H.R. Tillotson, 'Vincent J. Esch and the Architecture of Hyderabad, 1914–36', *South Asian Studies*, vol. IX (1993), pp. 29–46.

46 See Raymond Head, *The Indian Style* (London, 1986), p. 79.

47 See Tillotson, 1989, p. 61.

48 Some of Esch's drawings are preserved in the OIOC, British Library, and published in Tillotson, 1993.

49 JSPWD report 1884, pp. 78–9.

50 JSPWD report 1872, p. 5.

51 All Saints' is located to the south-west of the walled city; see Yaduendra Sahai, 'All Saint's Church: A Landmark', *The Times of India* (Jaipur, 25 December 1986), p. 3.

52 JSPWD report 1883, pp. 24, 73. The work involved the addition of a veranda to the Phul Mahal and the redecoration of the ceiling of the Sukh Nivas.

53 JSPWD report 1884, p. 13; and 1885, p. 9; Imarat works report 1884, p. 14.

54 This sequence can be deduced from the pattern of the stone courses of the platform.

55 JSPWD report 1881, p. 5.

56 For example, JSPWD report 1888.

57 Gordon Sanderson, *Types of Modern Indian Buildings* (Allahabad, 1913), p. 19.

58 JSPWD report 1893, p. 85; 1894, p. 11 and 1895, p. 7.

59 JSPWD report 1895, p. 7.

60 JSPWD report 1894, p. 10 and 1895, p. 7.

61 JSPWD report 1896, p. 7.

62 Quoted in Maharaja of Baroda, *The Palaces of India* (London, 1980), p. 156.

63 For details of his career, see especially, Y. P. Singh, ed., *Son of the Soil: Maharaja Ganga Singh* (Bikaner, 1981).

64 Rima Hooja, *Prince, Patriot, Parliamentarian: Biography of Dr Karni Singh, Maharaja of Bikaner* (New Delhi, 1997), p. 18.

65 The construction of these parts is discussed and illustrated in Sanderson, 1913, p. 15.

66 Sanderson, 1913, p. 16.

67 See Jon Lang, Madhavi Desai and Miki Desai, *Architecture and Independence: The Search for Identity 1880–1980* (New Delhi, 1997), p. 101. The university incorporated Muir College, whose building had been designed by Emerson in 1870.

68 JSPWD report 1894, p. 10. St Stephen's old building is near Kashmiri Gate and should not be confused with the 1934 building by Walter George.

69 JSPWD report 1901, p. 10.

70 JSPWD report 1902, p. 24; Showers, 1916, p. 67.

71 JSPWD report 1903–4, p. 20 and 1905–6, p. 44.

72 Robert Grant Irving, *Indian Summer: Lutyens, Baker and Imperial Delhi* (London, 1981), pp. 97–8.

73 Davies, 1985, pp. 203–4. Some sources attribute the design entirely to Jacob; see Lang, Desai and Desai, 1997, p. 101.

74 The building is dated by an inscription in the portico.

75 JSPWD report 1904–5, p. 3 and 1906–7, p. 18.

76 JSPWD report 1885, p. 3 and 1901, p. 4. In the following years the PWD reports continue to provide information about the work of the Raj Imarat.

77 The date follows A. K. Roy, *History of the Jaipur City* (New Delhi, 1978), appx VI, no. 50, p. 232. The attribution to Chiman Lal is supported by Sanderson, 1913, p. 17. This building is sometimes wrongly attributed to Jacob; but see the argument in Tillotson, 1989, pp. 77–8. See also Rahul Mehrotra, ed., *World Architecture: A Critical Mosaic, 1900–2000*, vol. VIII, *South Asia* (New York, 2001), pp. 4–5.

78 Sanderson, 1913, p. 18. See also Showers, 1916, p. 18, who uses the corrupt form 'Saraj ki Deorhi' which he translates as 'screen gate'.

79 Jain and Jain, eds, 1935, XVII, p. 3.

80 Sanderson, 1913, p. 18.

81 JSPWD report 1911–12, p. 21; 1912–13, p. 25; 1914–15, p. 29 and 1915–16, p. 19. The building houses a police station.

82 Showers, 1916, p. 44.

83 Ibid., p. 45.

84 JSPWD report 1908–9, p. 12; 1909–10, p. 17; 1911–12, p. 21; 1912–13, p. 25; 1914–15, p. 29 and 1915–16, p. 19; see also Showers, 1916, p. 46. The supposition that Jacob was a freelance when he worked on the design is based on the absence of any reference to the work in his PWD reports. Later, Stotherd's PWD reports continue to chart the activities of the Raj Imarat.

85 There is no marked entrance on the eastern garden front; the entrance was through a veranda facing the former garden on the west. See Showers, 1916, p. 45.

86 Jain and Jain, eds, 1935, XVII, p. 5; Roy, 1978, appx VI, no. 54, p. 232; Aman Nath, *Jaipur: The Last Destination* (Bombay, 1993), p. 101.

87 Gayatri Devi, *A Princess Remembers*, 3rd edn (Ghaziabad, 1983), pp. 151 ff; Nath, 1993, p. 101.

5 DELIVERING THE PAST

1 Rajiv Khanna, 'Rehabilitation of Bagore ki Haveli', *Architecture + Design*, vol. XVII/6 (2000), p. 77.

2 Jaipur Development Authority, *Jaipur Region Building Bye-Laws* (Jaipur, 1996), pp. 5–6.

3 Ibid., p. 14.

4 Ibid., pp. 9–10.

5 Ibid., p. 21.

6 Ibid., p. 39.

7 Kurula Varkey, 'The Essence of the Indian Tradition', *Architecture + Design*, vol. XVII/4 (2000), p. 98.

8 Ibid., pp. 98–102.

9 For example, William Curtis, *Balkrishna Doshi: An Architecture for India* (Ahmadabad, 1988); Hasan-Uddin Khan, *Charles Correa: Architect in India*, 2nd edn (London, 1987); Vikramaditya Prakash, 'Identity Production in Postcolonial Indian Architecture', *Postcolonial Space(s)*, ed. G. B. Nalbantoglu and C. T. Wong (New York, 199, pp. 38–52.

10 Curtis, 1988, p. 44.

11 *Marg*, vol. XLVIII/3 (1997).

12 Curtis, 1988, pp. 44–5.

13 Doshi in Curtis, 1988, p. 167.

14 Ibid., p. 44.

15 Ibid., p. 146.

16 B. V. Doshi, 'The Biocentric Essence', *Architecture + Design*, vol. XIV/1 (1997), p. 47.

17 Ibid., p. 46.

18 K. T. Ravindran, 'An Uncomfortable Glance at the Mirror', *Architecture + Design*, vol. XIV/1 (1997), p. 28.

19 Lalit Kala Akademi, *Seminar on Architecture* (Delhi, 1959), p. 48.

20 Charles Correa, 'The Public, the Private and the Sacred', *Architecture + Design*, VIII/5 (1991), p. 95.

21 Ibid., p. 95.

22 Ibid., p. 96.

6 THE USES OF *VASTU VIDYA*

1 P. K. Acharya, *Hindu Architecture in India and Abroad* (Calcutta, 1946).

2 See for an example of Brown's continuing influence, Christopher Tadgell, *The History of Architecture in India* (London, 1990).

3 Anna L. Dallapiccola, ed., *Shastric Traditions in Indian Arts*, 2 vols (Stuttgart, 1989); see the remarks of T. S. Maxwell, vol. I, pp. 5ff.

4 Vibhuti Chakrabarti, *Indian Architectural Theory* (London, 1998), pp. 12–13.

5 Gordon Sanderson, *Types of Modern Indian Buildings* (Allahabad, 1913).

6 For an account of the rise of the architectural profession in India, see Norma Evenson, *The Indian Metropolis: A View Toward the West* (New Haven, 1989), pp. 165 ff.

7 For fuller accounts of architecture and the transfer of power, see Vikram Bhatt and Peter Scriver, *After the Masters: Contemporary Indian Architecture* (Ahmadabad, 1990), and Jon Lang, Madhavi Desai and Miki Desai, *Architecture and Independence: The Search for Identity 1880–1980* (New Delhi, 1997).

8 For example, Norma Evenson, *Chandigarh* (Berkeley and Los Angeles, 1966); Sten Nilsson, *The New Capitals of India, Pakistan and Bangladesh* (repr. London, 1973); Sunand Prasad 'Le Corbusier in India', *Le Corbusier: Architect of the Century* (London, 1987), pp. 278–337; and Ravi Kalia, *Chandigarh: In Search of an Identity* (Carbondale, 1987).

9 See G.H.R. Tillotson, 'Architecture and Anxiety: The Problem of Pastiche in Recent Indian Design', *South Asia Research*, vol. XV/1 (1995), pp. 30–47; and Chakrabarti, 1998, chap. 7.

10 See Carmen Kagal, ed., *Vistara*, *The Architecture of India* (Bombay, 1986) and Tillotson, 1995.

11 See Brian Brace Taylor, *Raj Rewal* (London, 1992), pp. 21 and 26; and Raj Rewal et al., eds, *Architecture in India* (Paris, 1985).

12 For further discussion of this distinction see Chakrabarti, 1998, p. 86.

13 See for example Gouru Tirupati Reddy, *The Secret World of Vaasthu* (Proddatur, AP, 1994); Dharnidhar Sharma, *Dharnidhar's Vastu Guide* (Bombay, 1994); Derebail

Muralidhar Rao, *Hidden Treasures of Vastu Shilpa Shastra and Indian Traditions* (Bangalore, 1996).

14 For example, *Bhubanapadripa* discusses the style that is typical of Orissa; see Nirmal Kumar Bose, *Canons of Orissan Architecture* (repr. Delhi, 1982).

15 See the argument about ritual practice and meaning expounded in Caroline Humphrey and James Laidlaw, *The Archetypal Actions of Ritual* (Oxford, 1994).

Glossary

Between Sanskrit, standard modern Hindi, and conventional English spellings, it is not always possible to be consistent in transliteration. We have generally preferred the most familiar forms, and have not used diacritics.

alind अलिन्द veranda, gallery or portico

araish आराइश Jaipur wet fresco

avatar अवतार incarnation

ayurveda आयुर्वेद Indian system of medicine

bangaldar बंगलदार curved roof form, resembling the Bengali thatched roof

brahmasthana ब्रह्मस्थान central space presided over by Brahma, the divine creator

chaugan चौगान polo ground

chaupar चौपड़ cross roads (literally 'four-folded')

chhajja छज्जा sunshade, dripstone

chhatri छत्री small open pavilion, typically with four to eight columns supporting a dome (literally 'umbrella')

chowkri चौकड़ी ward (literally 'square section')

danda दण्ड unit of measurement roughly equal to *c.* 2 m

darbar दरबार royal congregation

gaddi गद्दी seat or throne

garbha griha गर्भ गृह part of a temple where the idol is placed, also a covered inner courtyard, (literally 'womb house')

geru गेरू powder of burnt bricks, terracotta, also the saffron colour of holy garb

gopura गोपुर gate-tower

guru गुरु teacher and spiritual guide

hasta हस्त unit of measurement roughly equivalent to *c.* 45 cm

haveli हवेली a generic name for a house constructed around courtyards

jali जाली pierced screen or trellis (literally 'mesh')

jati जाति class

jharokha झरोखा projecting window

jyotish vidya ज्योतिषविद्या Indian system of astrology

khat खत dado panel

mandala मण्डल organizing principle, graphically represented as a square or a circle

mistri मिस्तरी head mason, or craftsman

mohalla मुहल्ला community-based sub-division of a town or a city

murti मूर्ति idol, image of deity

nagara नागर north Indian (of architectural style)

pak vidya पाक विद्या Indian system of cooking

pandit पण्डित priest (literally 'learned one')

pradakshina patha प्रदक्षिणा पथ circumambulatory path around the deity

puja पूजा prayer, ritual

raga राग a composition in Indian classical music

rajmarg राजमार्ग principal street (literally 'royal path')

rasa रस mood (literally 'juice')

sarahad सरहद boundary, edge

sawai सवाई one and a quarter

shala शाला room or range under a single roof form

shastra शास्त्र canonical treatise

sheesh mahal शीश महल palace of mirrors

shikhara शिखर spire

takabandi ताकबन्दी visual response of echo

thakur ठाकुर noble of a Rajput court, ruler of a *thikana*

thikana ठिकाना district within a Rajput state, domain of a *thakur*

vastu वास्तु consecrated space, as in architecture, sculpture or painting

vastu purusha वास्तुपुरुष male principle of consecrated space

vastu shastra वास्तुशास्त्र generic name for treatises dealing with architecture

vastu vidya वास्तुविद्या Indic system of architecture (literally 'architectural knowledge')

vedh वेध violation (literally 'obstacle')

Select Bibliography

JAIPUR

Asopa, Jai Narayan, ed. *Cultural Heritage of Jaipur* (Jaipur, 1982)

Bahura, Gopal Narayan, ed., *Catalogue of the Manuscripts in the Maharaja of Jaipur Museum* (Jaipur, 1971)

—, *Literary Heritage of the Rulers of Amber and Jaipur* (Jaipur, 1976)

—, ed., *Ramavilasakavyam by Vishwanath Bhatt C. Ranade* (Jaipur, 1978)

—, ed., *Sawai Jaisingh Charita by Kavi Atmaram* (Jaipur, 1979)

—, ed., *Pratap Prakasa by Krishnadatta Kavi* (Jaipur, 1983)

— and Chandramani Singh, *Catalogue of Historical Documents in Kapad Dwara, Jaipur: Maps and Plans* (Jaipur, 1990)

Baylay, C. A., 'Jaipur', *The Rajputana Gazetteer*, vol. II (Calcutta, 1879), pp. 125–66

Bhatnagar, V. S., *Life and Times of Sawai Jai Singh 1688–1743* (Delhi, 1974)

Carapetian, Michael, 'Jaipur: The Pink City', *Architectural Review*, vol. CLXXII/1027 (1982), pp. 35–43

Devi, Gayatri, and Santha Rama Rao, *A Princess Remembers*, 3rd edn (Ghaziabad, 1983)

Dhama, B. L., *A Guide to Jaipur and Amber*, 2nd edn (Jaipur, 1955)

Erdman, Joan L., *Patrons and Performers in Rajasthan* (Delhi, 1985)

—, 'Jaipur: City Planning in 18th-century India', *Shastric Traditions in Indian Arts*, ed. Anna L. Dallapiccola *et al.*, 2 vols (Stuttgart, 1989), vol. I, pp. 219–35

Garrett, A.ff., and Chandradhar Guleri, *The Jaipur Observatory and its Builder* (Allahabad, 1902)

Hendley, Thomas Holbein, *London Indo-Colonial Exhibition of 1886: Handbook of the Jeypore Courts* (Calcutta, 1886)

—, *Memorials of the Jeypore Exhibition 1883* (Jaipur, 1893)

—, *Handbook of the Jeypore Museum* (Delhi, 1896) [1896a]

—, *Catalogue of the Collections of the Jeypore Museum*, 2 vols (Delhi, 1896) [1896b]

Jacob, Sir Samuel Swinton, *The Jeypore Portfolio of Architectural Details*, 12 vols (London, 1890–1913)

Jain, Kesharlal Ajmera, and Jawaharlal Jain, eds, *The Jaipur Album* (Jaipur, 1935)

Jaipur Development Authority, *Jaipur Region Building Bye-Laws* (Jaipur, 1996)

Jeypore State Public Works Reports (1868–1919)

Kaye, G. R., *The Astronomical Observatories of Jai Singh* (Calcutta, 1918)

Maharaja Sawai Man Singh II Museum; Drawings Collection

Marg, vol. XXX/4 (Bombay, 1977)

Michell, George, 'The Plan of Jaipur', *Storia della Città*, vol. VII (1978), pp. 64–8

Nath, Aman, *Jaipur: The Last Destination* (Bombay, 1993)

Newell, H. A., *Jaipur: The Astronomer's City* (London, 1915)

Nilsson, Sten, 'Jaipur, In the Sign of Leo', *Magasin Tessin*, no. 1 (1987)

—, 'Jaipur: Reflections of a Celestial Order', *Aspects of Conservation in Urban India*, ed. S. Nilsson (Lund, 1995), pp. 107–28

Pareek, Nand Kishore, *Jaipur That Was* (Jaipur, 2000)

Prakash, Vikramaditya, 'Identity Production in Postcolonial Indian Architecture', *Postcolonial Space(s)*, ed. G. B. Nalbantoglu and C. T. Wong (New York, 1997), pp. 38–52

Roy, Ashim Kumar, *History of the Jaipur City* (New Delhi, 1978)

Sahai, Yaduendra, 'Pink City: Its Original Colour and Allied Problems', *Cultural Contours of India*, ed. Vijai Shankar Srivastava (New Delhi, 1981), pp. 396–400

—, *Maharaja Sawai Ram Singh II of Jaipur: The Photographer Prince* (Jaipur, 1996)

Sarkar, Sir Jadunath, *A History of Jaipur c. 1503–1938*, ed. Raghubir Sinh (Hyderabad, 1984)

Sen, Opendro Nauth, *Report of the Jeypore School of Arts* (Jaipur, 1878)

Sharma, Hanuman, *Jaypur Rajya ka Itihas* (1937, repr. Jaipur, 1996)

Sharma, M. L., *History of the Jaipur State* (Jaipur, 1969)

Sharma, V. N., *Sawai Jai Singh and his Observatories* (Jaipur, 1977)

Showers, H. L., *Notes on Jaipur*, 2nd edn (Jaipur, 1916)

Stern, Robert W., *The Cat and the Lion: Jaipur State in the British Raj* (Leiden, 1988)

RAJASTHAN

Anand, Uma, *Mansions of the Sun: The Indian Desert Thaar* (London, 1982)

Adams, Archibald, *The Western Rajputana States* (London, 1899)

Agarawala, R. A., *Marwar Murals* (Delhi, 1977)

—, *History, Art and Architecture of Jaisalmer* (Delhi, 1979)

Banerjee, A. C., *The Rajput States and British Paramountcy* (New Delhi, 1980)

Beach, Milo Cleveland, *Mughal and Rajput Painting* (Cambridge, 1992)

Bhati, Narayan Singh, ed., *Marwar ra Pargana ri Vigat* (Jodhpur, 1968)

Chandra, Satish, *et al.*, eds, *Hukumat ri Bahi* (Delhi, 1976)

Chundawat, Lakshmi Kumari, *Sanskritik Rajasthan* (Jaipur, 1994)

Cimino, Rosa Maria, ed., *Life at Court in Rajasthan* (Florence, 1985)

Dadlich, Nityanand, ed., *Ajitodhaya Mahakavyam* (Jodhpur, 1980)

Desai, Vishakha N., ed., *Life at Court: Art for India's Rulers, 16th–19th Centuries* (Boston, 1985)

Goetz, Hermann, *The Art and Architecture of Bikaner State* (Oxford, 1950)

—, *Rajput Art and Architecture*, ed. Jyotindra Jain and Jutta Jain-Neubauer (Wiesbaden, 1978)

Hendley, Thomas Holbein, *The Rulers of India and the Chiefs of Rajputana* (London, 1897)

Hooja, Rima, *Prince, Patriot, Parliamentarian: Biography of Dr Karni Singh, Maharaja of Bikaner* (New Delhi, 1997)

Humphrey, Caroline, and James Laidlaw, *The Archetypal Actions of Ritual: A Theory of Ritual Illustrated by the Jain Rite of Worship* (Oxford, 1994)

Jain, K. C., *Ancient Cities and Towns of Rajasthan* (Delhi, 1972)

Joshi, M. C., *Dig* (New Delhi, 1982)

Khan, Shaukat Ali, *History and Historians of Rajasthan* (Delhi, 1982)

Kreisel, Gerd, *et al.*, *Rajasthan: Land der Konige* (Stuttgart, 1995)

Nath, Aman, and Francis Wacziarg, *Rajasthan: The Painted Walls of Shekhavati* (New Delhi, 1982)

—, eds, *Arts and Crafts of Rajasthan* (London, 1987)

Reu, Bisheshwar Nath, *Glories of Marwar and the Glorious Rathors* (Jodhpur, 1943)

Sarda, Har Bilas, *Maharana Kumbha: Sovereign, Soldier, Scholar* (Ajmer, 1932)

Sehgal, K. K., *Bikaner* [Rajasthan District Gazetteers] (Jaipur, 1972)

Sharma, Dasharatha, *Lectures on Rajput History and Culture* (Delhi, 1970)

Sharma, G. D., *Rajput Polity: A Study of Politics and Administration of the State of Marwar, 1638–1749* (Delhi, 1977)

Sharma, G. N., *Mewar and the Mughal Emperors* (Agra, 1954)

—, *Social Life in Medieval Rajasthan* (Agra, 1968)

Singh, Y. P., ed., *Son of the Soil: Maharaja Ganga Singh* (Bikaner, 1981)

Tillotson, G.H.R., *The Rajput Palaces: The Development of an Architectural Style, 1450–1750* (London, 1987)

—, ed., *Stones in the Sand: The Architecture of Rajasthan* (Mumbai, 2001)

Tod, James, *Annals and Antiquities of Rajast'han*, 2 vols (1829–32; repr. London, 1972)

Topsfield, Andrew, *Paintings from Rajasthan in the National Gallery of Victoria* (Melbourne, 1980)

—, *The City Palace Museum, Udaipur: Paintings of Mewar Court Life* (Ahmadabad, 1990)

VASTU VIDYA AND RELATED TEXTS

Acharya, P.K., *Architecture of Manasara*, Manasara series, vol. IV (1934; repr.Delhi, 1980)

—, *Hindu Architecture in India and Abroad* (Calcutta, 1946)

Achyuthan, A., and B.T.S. Prabhu, trans., *Manusyalayacandrika of Tirumangalat Nilakanthan Musat*, (Calicut, 1998)

Ayatattva Vishvakarma (Baroda and Ahmedabad, 1896)

Bhatt, Ramakrishna, trans., *Brihatsamhita of Varahamihira* (Delhi, 1987)

Bhattacharya, Tarapada, *The Canons of Indian Art: A Study of Vastuvidya* (1947; repr. Calcutta, 1963)

Boner, Alice, *et al.*, *Vastu Sutra Upanisad: The Essence of Form in Sacred Art* (New Delhi, 1982)

Bose, Nirmal Kumar, *Canons of Orissan Architecture* (1932; repr. Delhi, 1982)

Bose, P. N., trans., *Silpasastram*, Punjab Oriental series, no. 17 (Lahore, 1928)

Chakrabarti, Vibhuti [Sachdev], *Indian Architectural Theory: Contemporary Uses of Vastu Vidya* (London, 1998)

Dagens, Bruno, trans., *Mayamata: An Indian Treatise on Housing, Architecture and Iconography* (Delhi, 1985)

— (trans.), *Mayamatam: Treatise of Housing, Architecture and Iconography*, 2 vols (New Delhi, 1994)

Dallapiccola, Anna Libera, ed., *Shastric Traditions in Indian Arts*, 2 vols, (Stuttgart, 1989)

Doniger, Wendy, trans., *The Laws of Manu* (London, 1991)

Dubey, Lal Mani, *Aparajita Priccha: A Critical Study* (Allahabad, 1987)

Dvivedi, Ramanihor, trans., and Brahmananda Tripathi, ed., *Brihadvastumala*, Chowkhamba Surabharati Granthamala 12, 4th edn (Benares, 1992)

Dvivedi, Vindhyeshvariprasad , trans, *Vasturatnakara*, Haridas Sanskrit Granthamala 46, 5th edn (Benares, 1988)

Gopal, Lallanji, *The Sukraniti: A Nineteenth-century Text*, Bharati Prakashan (Varanasi, 1978)

Growse, F. S., trans., *The Ramayana of Tulasidas*, rev. R. C. Prasad (Delhi, 1978)

Jain, Bhagvanadas (trans.), *Vastusara Prakarna of* Chandrangaj Thakkur Pheru, Jaina Vividha Granthamala, no. 3 (Jaipur, 1939)

Jain, Bhagvandas trans., *Paramjain Chandrangaj Thakkur 'Pheru' Virachit Vastusar Prakaran*, Shri Digambar Jain Atishay Kshetra Mandir Sanghji Janganer (Jaipur, 1997)

Jain, Bhagvandas, trans., *Sutradhar Mandan Virachit Prasad Mandan*, Shri Digambar Jain Atishay Kshetra Mandir Sanghji Sanganer (Jaipur, 1997)

Jha, Jivananatha. ed., and Achyutnanda Jha. trans., *Vasturatnavali*, Haridas Sanskrit series no. 152, 3rd edn (Benares, 1971)

Jha, Pt. Achyutnandana, trans., *Brihatsamhita of Varahamihira*, Chowkamba Vidyabhavana (Benares, 1993)

Kangle, R. P., trans., *The Kautiliya Arthasastra*, part 2 (repr. Delhi, 1972)

Kramrisch, Stella, *The Hindu Temple*, 2 vols (1946; repr. Delhi, 1991)

Krishnadas, Khemaraja Shri, trans., *Vishvakarmaprakasha* (Bombay, 1988)

Mallaya, N.V., *Studies in Sanskrit Texts on Temple Architecture with Special Reference to Tantrasamuccay* (Annamalai 1949)

Mihirchand, Pandit, trans., *Vishvakarma Prakash*, Khemraj Shrikrishnadas (Bombay, 1988)

Mishra, Acharya Ramajanma (trans.), *Naradasamhita*, Kashi Sanskrit Granthamala 40, 3rd edn (Benares, 1995)

Ojha, Ramyatna, trans., and Madhavaprasada Vyasa, rev., *Vasturajavallabha of Mandana Sutradhara*, 2nd edn (Benares, 1934)

Pandeya, Matriprasada, trans., *Vastumanikya Ratnakara*, 3rd edn (Benares, 1983)

Pillai, Govinda Krishna, *The Ways of the Silpis* (Allahabad, 1948)

Raz, Ram, *An Essay on the Architecture of the Hindus* (London, 1834)

Sarkar, B. K., trans., *The Sukraniti* (1st edn, 1914; repr. New Delhi, 1975)

Shastri, Nemichandra, *Bhartiya Jyotisha*, Bhartiya Gyanapitha (1952; repr. Delhi, 1994)

Shastri, Siyasharan, *Shrisitaramji Ke Mandir Ka Itihas Evam Utsav Mala*, Shriramjanaki Devi (Jaipur, 1994)

Shukla, D. N., *Vastu-Sastra* (2 vols, 1958–60; repr. New Delhi, 1993)

—, trans., *Samarangana Sutradhara* (Delhi, 1994)

Shukla, Shaktidhara and Munshi Palarama, ed., *Vishvakarmaprakasha*, Palarama Vilasa (Lucknow, 1896)

INDIAN ARCHITECTURAL HISTORY

Aga Khan Award for Architecture, *Regionalism and Architecture* (Cambridge, MA, 1985)

Allen, Charles, and Sharada Dwivedi, *Lives of the Indian Princes* (London, 1984)

Barringer, Tim, and Tom Flynn, eds, *Colonialism and the Object: Empire, Material Culture and the Museum* (London, 1998)

Bhatt, Vikram, and Peter Scriver, *After the Masters: Contemporary Indian Architecture* (Ahmadabad, 1990)

Brown, Percy, *Indian Architecture*, 2 vols (Bombay, 1942)

Case, Margaret H., ed., *Govindadeva: A Dialogue in Stone* (New Delhi, 1996)

Curtis, William, *Balkrishna Doshi: An Architecture for India* (Ahmedabad, 1988)

Davies, Philip, *Splendours of the Raj: British Architecture in India 1660–1947* (London, 1985)

Evenson, Norma, *Chandigarh* (Berkeley and Los Angeles, 1966)

—, *The Indian Metropolis: A View toward the West* (New Haven, 1989)

Fergusson, James, *History of Indian and Eastern Architecture*, 2 vols (1876; rev. London, 1910)

Gole, Susan, *Indian Maps and Plans* (New Delhi, 1989)

Guy, John, and Deborah Swallow, eds, *Arts of India, 1550–1900* (London, 1990)

Hardy, Adam, *Indian Temple Architecture: Form and Transformation* (New Delhi, 1994)

Havell, E. B., *Indian Architecture* (1st edn, 1913; 2nd edn, London, 1927)

Head, Raymond, *The Indian Style* (London, 1986)

Irving, Robert Grant, *Indian Summer: Lutyens, Baker and Imperial Delhi* (London, 1981)

Kagal, Carmen, ed., *Vistara, The Architecture of India* (Bombay, 1986)

Kalia, Ravi, *Chandigarh: In Search of an Identity* (Carbondale, 1987)

Khan, Hasan-Uddin, *Charles Correa: Architect in India*, 2nd edn (London, 1987)

Lalit Kala Akademi, *Seminar on Architecture* (Delhi, 1959)

Lang, Jon, Madhavi Desai and Miki Desai, *Architecture and Independence: The Search for Identity 1880–1980* (New Delhi, 1997)

Mehrotra, Rahul, ed., *World Architecture: A Critical Mosaic 1900–2000*, vol. VIII, *South Asia* (New York, 2001)

Metcalf, Thomas R., *An Imperial Vision: Indian Architecture and Britain's Raj* (London, 1989)

Michell, George, and Antonio Martinelli, *The Royal Palaces of India* (London, 1994)

Nilsson, Sten, *The New Capitals of India, Pakistan and Bangladesh* (1973; repr. London, 1978)

Pramar, V. S., *Haveli: Wooden Houses and Mansions of Gujarat* (Ahmadabad, 1989)

Reuther, Oscar, *Indische Paläste und Wohnhäuser* (Berlin, 1925)

Rousselet, Louis, *India and its Native Princes*, trans. Lt.-Col. Buckle (London, 1876)

Ray, Amita, *Villages, Towns and Secular Buildings in Ancient India* (Calcutta, 1964)

Rewal, Raj, *et al.*, eds, *Architecture in India* (Paris, 1985)

Sanderson, Gordon, *Types of Modern Indian Buildings* (Allahabad, 1913)

Sealey, Neil E., *Planned Cities in India* (London, 1982)

Sugich, Michael, *Palaces of India* (London, 1992)

Tadgell, Christopher, *The History of Architecture in India: From the Dawn of Civilization to the End of the Raj* (London, 1990)

Taylor, Brian Brace, *Raj Rewal* (London, 1992)

Tillotson, G.H.R., *The Tradition of Indian Architecture: Continuity, Controversy and Change since 1850* (London, 1989)

Toy, Sidney, *The Fortified Cities of India* (London, 1965)

Vale, Lawrence J., *Architecture, Power and National Identity* (London, 1992)

Volwahsen, Andreas, *Architecture of the World: India* (Lausanne, 1968)

Index